Health Care for the Indigent and Competitive Contracts

The Arizona Experience

Health Care for the Indigent and Competitive Contracts

The Arizona Experience

Jon B. Christianson
Diane G. Hillman

HEALTH ADMINISTRATION PRESS PERSPECTIVES

Ann Arbor, Michigan   1986

Library of Congress Cataloging-in-Publication Data

Christianson, Jon B.
    Health care for the indigent and competitive contracts.

    Includes index.
    1. Poor—Medical care—Arizona—Finance. 2. Medical care—Arizona—Contracting out. 3. Contracts, Letting of—Arizona. 4. Public contracts—Arizona. I. Hillman, Diane G. II. Title. [DNLM: 1. Cost Control—methods. 2. Financial Management—organization and administration. 3. Medical Assistance—Economics—Arizona. 4. Medical Indigency. W 250 C555h]
RA418.5.P6C48   1986   362.1'04252   86-4643
ISBN 0-910701-12-1 (pbk.)

Health Administration Press
School of Public Health
The University of Michigan
1021 East Huron
Ann Arbor, Michigan 48109
(313) 764-1380

Health Administration Press
Perspectives is an imprint of Health
Administration Press dedicated to
books and other material of timely
and special interest for health
care practitioners.

J we
2-19-88

Contents

Preface

It is unusual to be able to study close at hand a major experiment in health policy as it unfolds on a day-to-day basis. The passage of the Arizona Health Care Cost Containment System (AHCCCS) in October 1981 provided us this opportunity. Our study was guided by an initial decision to focus our efforts on the competitive bidding aspect of the Arizona experiment. In our judgment the proposed competitive bidding process represented the major innovation in the legislation and promised to have the most far-reaching implications for health policy in the United States.

In addition to the opportunity the Arizona legislation offered for an analysis of competitive bidding for medical care contracts, we were fortunate to be granted the requisite financial support for our research. Grants from the John A. Hartford Foundation of New York City, New York and the Flinn Foundation of Phoenix, Arizona allowed us to devote a substantial portion of our time to the research between June 1982 and June 1984. This support permitted us to examine all aspects of the bidding process and its ramifications at a breadth and level of detail that otherwise would not have been possible. We are very grateful for this support, as well as the encouragement of John Billings, Patricia Drury, and John Murphy.

While both opportunity and financial support facilitated our research efforts, we could not have conducted the analysis at any level without the cooperation of individuals throughout the state of Arizona. Essential data for the study were collected through interviews with medical care providers, legislators, legislative staff, personnel in the Arizona Department of Health Services, and employees of McAuto Systems Group, Inc. Because of the large number of interviews, it is not possible to acknowledge all of these individuals by name. However, their willingness to discuss freely their ideas, motivations, and actions made the research possible. In addition to information collected through interviews, we relied heavily on position papers, memoranda, and other documents supplied by the AHCCCS Division in the Arizona Department of Health Services to establish key dates and facts. In this regard, we especially appreciate the efforts of Ken Bohaty, Steve Brooks, William Chamberlain, Dr. Henry Foley, Fred Meister, Robert Schneider, and Aldona Vaitkus.

Finally, we wish to thank our colleagues Kenneth Smith, Bradford Kirkman-Liff, and Nicholas Aquilano for their participation in various portions of this research project, as well as Vernon Greene and Ronald Vogel for their encouragement and criticism. While their views are not necessarily represented in this book, they were important in stimulating our thinking about numerous aspects of the competitive bidding process.

Jon B. Christianson
Diane G. Hillman

June 1984

List of Figures and Tables

Figures

Tables

x   *List of Figures and Tables*

Abbreviations

ADHS	Arizona Department of Health Services
AFDC	Aid to Families with Dependent Children
AFP-IPA	Academy of Family Physicians IPA
AHCCCS	Arizona Health Care Cost Containment System
DES	Department of Economic Security
DHHS	Department of Health and Human Services
EPSDT	Early and Periodic Screening and Diagnostic Testing
HCFA	Health Care Financing Administration
HMO	Health Maintenance Organization
IPA	Independent Practice Association
JLOC	Joint Legislative Oversight Committee
MI	Medically Indigent
MN	Medically Needy
MSGI	McAuto Systems Group, Inc.
OMB	Office of Management and Budget
PHP	Prepaid Health Plan
RFP	Request for Proposal
TEFRA	Tax Equity and Fiscal Responsibility Act
VPR	Voluntary Price Reduction

1

Introduction: Competitive Contracting in Indigent Medical Care Programs

Rapid increases in expenditures within the Medicaid program by both state and federal governments have stimulated a variety of approaches to limit the open-ended nature of this program. Initially, states responded to increases in Medicaid program expenditures by attempting to limit the scope of services provided and tighten eligibility requirements. Recent changes in federal law, however, have created opportunities for states to control their medical care expenditures for indigents by restructuring the financial incentives for participating providers. State governments are currently exploring competitive bidding by providers for contracts to deliver specified sets of services to defined populations, with significant federal support and encouragement. Of all the states, Arizona has been the most aggressive in implementing competitive bidding in its indigent medical care program. As part of a three-year demonstration program, Arizona has relied on competitive bidding to establish a complete acute care delivery system for its indigent population and establish reimbursement rates for participating provider organizations. In this book we analyze the initial experience with competitive bidding for indigent medical care contracts in Arizona. Because of the ambitious and comprehensive nature of the Arizona competitive bidding process and the increasing popularity of competitive bidding in public medical care programs, our analysis has important implications for the development of health policy in other states and at the federal level.

The purpose of this introductory chapter is to place Arizona in the context of other efforts nationwide to change the structure of delivery systems for indigent medical care. First, we present a brief overview of the Arizona competitive bidding process. Then we discuss the rationale behind the demands of state Medicaid administrators for increased flexibility in the organization of their programs and describe federal responses to those demands. We also describe the initiatives for reform that have been undertaken by several states, as well as the nature of the Arizona experiment and how it relates to these initiatives.

An Overview of the Arizona Experiment in Competitive Contracting

In November of 1981, Arizona lawmakers enacted the Arizona Health Care Cost Containment System (AHCCCS). The AHCCCS legislation contained seven mechanisms intended to control program costs: (1) prepaid capitated financing, (2) capitation payments to the state by the federal government, (3) limitations on freedom of choice by consumers, (4) cost sharing by consumers, (5) primary care physicians acting as gatekeepers for all medical care, (6) competitive bidding to select a program administrator, and (7) competitive bidding to select medical care providers. This book focuses primarily on the experience of AHCCCS with competitive contracting with providers.

During the first round of bidding, program administrators followed the directives of the legislation in placing few limits on the provider organizations eligible to submit bids or the geographical areas covered by bids. However, several other features of the bidding process outlined in the legislation were modified in implementation. For instance, the legislation invited separate bids in four service categories (inpatient, outpatient, pharmacy, and laboratory and x-ray), but program administrators expressed a clear preference for bids covering all categories under one price ("full service bids"). Similarly, legislated population categories were respecified, and bids in some categories (including private and government employee groups) were effectively ignored in the awarding of contracts. Also, although the legislation allowed latitude for a two-year contract, initial contracts covered a single year.

In addition, program administrators made several important decisions concerning operational aspects of competitive bidding not directly addressed in the legislation. For example, program officials sought contractual capacity to serve a total number of indigents in each county that was equal to or in excess of the estimated number of indigents, and stated their preference for more than one winning bidder in a given area. They also agreed to reimburse each winning bidder the amount of its bid price, a standard practice in government procurement that had not been specified in the legislation.

After the first year of the program, some components of the bidding process were redefined. For instance, early and periodic screening and diagnostic treatment (EPSDT) services for children were added to service requirements, bids for private and government employee groups were no longer required, the composition of the population groups covered by different bids was redefined, and the "preference" for full service bids was changed to a requirement. At the time, these changes were regarded primarily as "technical adjustments" to the bidding process.

The initial round of bidding occurred between January and September of 1982. The first six months were devoted primarily to defining rules and regulations for the program, developing a waiver request for submission to Health Care Financing Administration (HCFA), and selecting a private firm to assume major program management responsibilities. However, the drafting of rules and regulations was not completed as scheduled, so bidding took place under "emergency" rules and regulations. In effect, bidding organizations were asked to commit themselves to a program that was not yet clearly defined. In addition, delays in hiring the administrative firm meant that the criteria for evaluating provider bids had not been developed prior to bid submission. Consequently, the AHCCCS competitive bidding process initially lacked both a definitive set of procedural rules and a well-understood set of criteria for the selection of winning bidders.

Despite these shortcomings, a Request for Proposals (RFP) for provider services was released on July 2, 1982. It contained a draft of the prototype provider contract, estimates of service utilization, population and costs for each county, lists of required services, a general description of factors which would be considered in the evaluation of bids, and forms to be completed in the calculation of bid prices. Thirty-nine full service bids were received from different organizations. Bids that were considered qualified and technically acceptable were ranked according to a composite price, which was essentially a weighted average of the bid prices for each population category, with weights determined by the estimated number of indigents per category.

AHCCCS officials determined that the program budget was insufficient to cover project enrollment and utilization at the prices bid in 6 of the 14 counties. The AHCCCS Division staff within the State Department of Health Services, representatives of the administrative firm, state legislators, and staff from the attorney general's office met to discuss possible solutions. Direct negotiation with bidders over their prices was rejected on the grounds that state procurement precedent did not allow such an approach. Instead, voluntary price reductions (VPRs) by bidders in the 6 counties were requested. It was suggested that, if the price reductions were insufficient to meet AHCCCS budget constraints, all bids in those counties would be rejected and providers would be asked to resubmit bids.

Contract offers were made to bidders in 8 counties and conditional contract offers, contingent on formal acceptance of price reductions were made in the remaining 6 counties. Eligibility determination for program enrollees began in all counties on September 1, as scheduled, and enrollment with providers began in the 8 counties with contract awards. The reductions offered by providers were subsequently judged acceptable, allowing enrollment in these counties. Although a significant number of details remained to be resolved before contracts with providers were formally signed, delivery of services by winning bidders began as scheduled on October 1, 1982.

In the second year of the program, the bidding cycle was initiated much earlier, with an invitation to bid issued on May 17. When bids were received, it was again determined that the state's budget would be exceeded if contracts were awarded at the bid prices submitted in all counties. As a result, officials repeated their first-round request for VPRs, with the rejection of all bids as an alternative if the reductions offered by providers were not sufficient. This time, however, the reductions offered by providers were not sufficient. In the remaining counties, a second invitation to bid was issued, and new bids were subsequently judged sufficiently low to allow the program to proceed in its second year.

The actual operation of the program during its initial two years was marked by several controversies. There were allegations that winning bidders delivered poor quality medical care and that the program was mismanaged by the state and its administrative contractor. The majority of winning bidders did not file the financial reports required by their contracts, nor did they implement the required quality assurance systems. The state's efforts to enforce compliance with contractual reporting requirements were sporadic at best during this initial period.

Financial Pressures on Indigent Medical Care

Between 1972 and 1977, Medicaid program costs rose from $6.2 billion to $16.3 billion, while the number of program enrollees increased from 17.6 million to 22.9 million. Although program expenditures for long-term care are growing rapidly, most Medicaid dollars continue to purchase acute medical care. Medicaid pays almost 10 percent of all hospital expenditures in the United States and accounts for a significantly larger proportion of reimbursements in university teaching hospitals. More important than the level of Medicaid expenditures is their relative growth rate: Overall Medicaid program costs increased 40 percent faster than total health care expenditures in the United States during the decade of the 1970s. In 1981, Medicaid outlays increased by 18 percent, and by 1982, spending had risen to $30 billion.[1] Expenditures for Medicaid in fiscal year 1983 totaled approximately $37 billion, with $19.5 billion contributed by the federal government and $17 billion by the states.

These rapidly increasing expenditures pose a serious problem for both state and federal governments, particularly since the ability of states to finance Medicaid programs has been decreasing in recent years. The Intergovernmental Health Policy Project reports that in January 1981 over 50 percent of the states projected "moderate to serious shortfalls in their Medicaid budgets." By May of that same year, "states reported significant deficits and 13 states found it necessary to rely on supplemental appropriations to cover expected deficits attributable to Medicaid alone." During 1981, 30 states made alterations in their Medicaid programs, including changes in benefits, eligibility, or provider reimbursement levels, in order to stay within their budgets.[2,3] Expenditures for Medicaid programs are greater than for any other single program financed by most state governments. Furthermore, the rate of increase of expenditures for medical care for the poor is growing more rapidly than for any other program.[4] And, the "growth in total revenues in most states has been far less than the average annual increase in Medicaid expenditures over the past few years."[5] Thus, the relationship between the services that Medicaid originally intended for indigents, and those that states now feel they can afford, has become a critical issue for state governments.

State governments are not alone in their concern about rising Medicaid expenditures; the Reagan administration initially targeted that program for major budget reductions. A proposal in March 1981 would have placed "an immediate and mandatory ceiling on federal Medicaid payments . . . and would have resulted in an estimated savings of $9 billion between 1983 and 1985."[6] In addition, states would have been given increased flexibility in the design of their Medicaid programs. While Congress did not accept this proposed federal ceiling, it did lower the federal matching rate by 3 percent in the Omnibus Budget Reconciliation Act of 1981. When combined with changes in Medicaid that were included in the Tax Equity and Fiscal Responsibility Act of 1982 (TEFRA), this law resulted in decreased rates of program expenditure increases. It was projected that the rate of increase in total program budgets would be cut from 15 percent (1975 to 1980) to 9.1 percent (1983 to 1984).[7] The Reagan administration is considering further steps to control federal Medicaid expenditure increases, including requirements for copayments for some services, improvement of collections from other payers, and extension of the 3 percent reduction in federal matching dollars beyond 1985. If adopted, the last proposal would put additional pressure on states to further restrain their own Medicaid expenditures.

Federal Legislation to Increase Flexibility in Program Design

The states' initial response to the increasing costs of their Medicaid programs was to reduce benefits, tighten eligibility requirements, limit reimbursements to providers, and improve program management.[8] Reductions in benefits, implemented in the majority of states, included restrictions on the number of covered inpatient hospital days (often defined by diagnosis), elimination of optional services (e.g., selected drugs, chiropractic care, eyeglasses, and pediatric care), limitation of reimbursements for inappropriate use of emergency and outpatient departments, and introduction of cost sharing for some groups of program participants. More stringent eligibility criteria have been used by some states to reduce the number of Medicaid enrollees.

Several states now exclude 18- to 21-year-old Aid to Families with Dependent Children (AFDC) recipients, while other states have reduced the upper limit on income in order to exclude more indigents.[9] Reductions in reimbursements of hospitals, nursing homes, and physicians have also been adopted in an effort to contain costs. Changes in administration and management of providers include increased fraud and abuse control, the "lock-in" of recipients to particular providers, the "lock-out" of providers who abuse the program, increased third-party liability recovery attempts, volume purchasing and competitive bidding for supplies, and more effective monitoring of utilization. Steps taken to control utilization have included requirements for prior authorization of services, second opinions for elective surgery, and prepayment review of hospital admissions and length of stay. Finally, the majority of states have requested waivers to allow funding of home and community-based services in an attempt to reduce dependence on costly nursing homes. Swing bed programs have been proposed in an effort to better utilize empty hospital beds, and some states have suggested the use of tax credits for care of the elderly and disabled at home or, conversely, requirements that families of Medicaid recipients share costs.

Most of these approaches to the control of Medicaid expenditures primarily represented modifications in the design and operation of existing programs. However, as Medicaid costs continued to accelerate, state program administrators sought greater flexibility in altering the fundamental design of programs and greater power to limit the freedom of program enrollees to choose their source of care. Congress responded to these state requests in two ways. First, under the Omnibus Reconciliation Act of 1981, states were allowed to apply for waivers from the previous Medicaid provision that all recipients have complete freedom of choice of provider. Second, states were granted waivers under Section 1115 of the Social Security Act to test a variety of "competitive approaches" to the delivery of care under the Medicaid program.

Omnibus Reconciliation Act of 1981

Provisions under Section 2175 of the Omnibus Reconciliation Act of 1981 (P.L. 97–35) allowed Medicaid program administrators great latitude in the selection of providers to serve enrollees. Under this act, a number of experiments in provider selection and reimbursement have resulted, with more likely in the future. As stated by

Senator Robert Dole, "We certainly intend to continue providing states with the flexibility necessary to allow them to improve program operations and service delivery. We may actually learn something from the Medicaid programs in their use of community based resources."[10]

The provisions of the Omnibus Reconciliation Act critical to the states' ability to test new cost containment programs are those that modify the long-standing requirement that Medicaid enrollees have complete freedom of choice to obtain services from qualified providers. There are two ways in which states can be exempted from these freedom-of-choice requirements under this act. First, states may use competitive bidding for laboratory and other services, or establish "lock-in" or "lock-out" programs for specified periods of time, to correct for overutilization by specific enrollees and to limit participation by costly providers, respectively.

Second, states may apply for waiver of state plan requirements that limit risk-sharing arrangements with federally qualified health maintenance organizations (HMOs). These waivers are intended to increase the number and types of provider groups that may participate in Medicaid programs. Section 1915(b) of the Social Security Act, under which waiver approval is required, has four subsections. Each provides the opportunity to create greater cost-consciousness on the part of various "actors."[11] Waivers may be granted under these four subsections for up to two years if the Secretary of DHHS considers them consistent with the goals of the Medicaid program and likely to be cost-effective and efficient. The four subsections of 1915(b) allow states or localities to

1. implement a primary care case management system
2. act as a central broker in assisting Medicaid recipients in selecting among competing health plans
3. share with recipients, through the provision of additional services, savings resulting from recipients' use of more cost-effective Medical care
4. restrict recipients to receiving services (other than in emergency situations) from only efficient and cost-effective providers.[12]

As of August 1982, 30 requests for waivers of the freedom-of-choice provisions had been submitted by 15 states to the Health Care Financing Administration (HCFA). Of these 30 requests, 60 percent attempted to set up primary care case management systems.[13] Also known as the "case management system," the primary care network model is composed of primary care physicians who serve as entry points for enrollees. All care, including hospitalizations and speciality referrals, is managed by these physicians, who are then responsible for the ultimate utilization of services by enrollees. Most often, in the Medicaid demonstrations proposed under this provision, the primary care physicians are placed "at some economic risk in an effort to make them more prudent consumers of medical resources."[14] The overall goal is to alter the practice behavior of these physicians, who are thought to initiate about 75 percent of medical care, by changing their reimbursement mechanism from fee-for-service to capitation payments. Physicians who choose to participate in such systems have reduced financial incentives to promote inappropriate or excessive levels of care, since they may be at risk for primary and specialty or hospital care.[15] The degree of risk faced by the physician varies considerably, depending on the likelihood of, and need for, participation by providers. For instance, physicians in Colorado's program may gain from cost-conscious practice but face no financial risk. Those from Michigan are under no risk but receive fee-for-service reimbursements plus care management fees, although excesses over target costs could result in future exclusion from the program.[16] There are several mechanisms under which the physician participants in primary care networks are identified, including competitive bidding for contracts, direct negotiation between the state and providers, prudent purchasing of services on a capitation basis by states and localities, and exclusion of providers with "high cost patient profiles" from participation in Medicaid, as in Michigan.[17]

Section 1915(b)(2), which would allow states and localities to assist members in selecting among competing health plans, has not been cited as the principal authority for waivers by any state, as of 1982. Several states have applied for waivers under Section 1915(b)(2), which allows states to provide additional benefits or exemptions to copayment requirements for enrollees using more cost-effective medical care.

Application for waivers under Section 1915(b)(4) of the Social Security Act is the final means by which a number of states have attempted to reduce costs. Under this authority, states may "restrict recipients to obtaining services from a provider or providers that have demonstrated effectiveness and efficiency in providing such services."[18] The potential savings from this approach are substantial. For instance, it was estimated by the General Accounting Office that restriction of Medicaid patients to low cost hospitals might save $1.6 million in Baltimore and $1.7 million in Atlanta.[19] However, potential problems in the design of such programs, including the effect on the geographical accessibility of program participants, resulted in the funding of several demonstrations to test a variety of approaches.

Section 1115 Waivers

Congress has also allowed states increased flexibility in the management of their Medicaid programs through the use of "competition demonstration projects" administered by the Health Care Financing Administration. Under Section 1115 of the Social Security Act, states may be granted waivers from many of the usual Medicaid requirements in order to test experimental approaches to the delivery of medical care. In March 1982, states were offered the opportunity, via a special solicitation by HCFA, to design and implement demonstration projects where competition between providers would be a key feature of program design. A total of 15 proposals were submitted by ten states, and five states were awarded grants to plan and implement projects to enhance competition within their Medicaid programs. Most of these projects have a one-year planning phase and a three-year demonstration phase. The states that responded to the 1982 solicitation and were awarded grants are Florida (Alternative Health Plan Project); Minnesota (Medicaid Voucher Demonstration); Missouri (Prepaid Health Demonstration Project, Kansas City area); New Jersey (Medicaid Competition Demonstration); and New York (MediCap Plan, Monroe County).[20]

The Arizona Health Care Cost Containment System (AHCCCS) was funded by the county, state, and federal governments under Title XIX of the Social Security Act. However, Section 1115 waivers were granted to Arizona to test a number of cost containment features prior to the solicitation described above. The key feature in the Arizona program that qualifies it for federal waivers is the use of a competitive bidding process to award contracts to providers, who act as primary care gatekeepers to deliver comprehensive medical care to program enrollees.

Comprehensive Statewide Experiments

The authority provided by the federal government, under the Omnibus Reconciliation Act of 1981 and Section 1115 of the Social Security Act, has resulted in two programs that are particularly comprehensive in nature: the California Selective Provider Contracting Program and the Arizona Health Care Cost Containment System. Both programs use competitive bidding by providers for contracts to deliver medical care to indigents. Both were the result of similar environmental influences: budgetary crises at the state level brought about by federal cutbacks, the economic recession, and limitations on state revenue-generating capacities (due to Proposition 13 in California); rapid increases in medical care costs statewide, due in part to excess numbers of hospital beds and physicians; and pressure on state legislatures from business and labor coalitions, faced with increasingly costly employee health care, that protested the "cost shifts" resulting from losses incurred by institutions caring for indigent patients in prior years.[21] In response to these pressures, both California and Arizona utilized the flexibility provided by the new federal provisions to make radical changes in their indigent medical care programs.

California

The Selective Provider Contracting Program was funded under Section 1915(b)(4) of the Social Security Act. California initially responded to the budget pressure described above by enacting a 6 percent limit on annual increases in hospital payments for its Medi-Cal enrollees. When a coalition of health care industry interests subsequently lobbied against the cap, the legislature responded with a bill (AB 799) which has been characterized as establishing "a system of competitive bidding for Medi-Cal beneficiaries."[22] In fact, the program resulting from the bill is a curious mixture of bidding and negotiation, with heavy emphasis on negotiation.

The California program is structured as a two-year experiment for which the federal government granted approval effective in October 1982. The key element of the experiment is the establishment of a Medi-Cal chief negotiator, authorized by legislation to negotiate with hospitals on behalf of the program. A former vice president of Southern California Blue Cross was appointed by the governor to the position of Medi-Cal "czar." This czar was replaced by the California Medical Assistance Commission on July 1, 1983, after one year in service, as planned.

The Medi-Cal czar began negotiations in urban communities with high concentrations of Medi-Cal patients by requesting hospitals to submit bids to provide inpatient care. On the basis of their initial bids, some hospitals were then contacted by the negotiation team.

According to Ensign and Mayerhofer, "No matter what price the hospital offered, the uniform response was 'knock off $50 and we'll reconsider your bid.'"[23] Through early 1983, contracts had been signed with hospitals in virtually all of California's more populous areas. The contracting hospitals were institutions that had provided about 75 percent of all Medi-Cal patient days in 1981. The target negotiated rate for these hospitals was their 1981 cost per diem minus 10 percent.

Arizona

The Arizona Health Care Cost Containment System (AHCCCS) was enacted in November 1981 and initiated in October 1982 as a three-year demonstration project to test a variety of approaches to health care cost containment, the primary one being competition among providers. Waivers under Section 1115 allowed receipt of Title XIX funds for the first time in Arizona, the only state that elected not to participate in the traditional Medicaid program. A brief overview of the Arizona experiment was presented earlier in this chapter. The next two chapters of this book describe the development of AHCCCS and the provisions of the law as enacted. Then, after a discussion in chapter 4 of issues in the design of competitive bidding systems for indigent medical care, we describe the development of the bidding system in AHCCCS in chapter 5. We then analyze the implementation process in chapter 6, with particular emphasis on the mechanisms used to transform a theoretical competitive bidding system into reality, and the resulting problems. Chapter 7 describes and evaluates the participation of providers in the AHCCCS bidding process, and chapter 8 analyzes the initial experience in the AHCCCS with contract enforcement and compliance. A concluding chapter discusses the lessons to be learned from the initial experience in Arizona with competitive bidding for indigent medical care contracts.

Notes

1. J. B. Christianson, K. R. Smith, and D. G. Hillman, "A Comparison of Existing and Alternative Competitive Bidding Systems for Indigent Medical Care," *Social Science and Medicine* 18 (1984): 599–604.
2. Intergovernmental Health Policy Project, "Recent and Proposed Changes in State Medicaid Programs—A Fifty State Survey," George Washington University, July 1982.

3. For example, the state of California faced a $2 billion deficit in its proposed budget for fiscal year 1982–1983 and an actual deficit of nearly $1 billion for 1981–1982. Of this deficit, about $1 of every $8 was attributable to the Medi-Cal program, California's version of Medicaid. E. P. Melia, L. M. Aucoin, L. H. Duhl, and P. S. Kurokawa, "Competition in the Health Care Marketplace: A Beginning in California," *New England Journal of Medicine* 308, no. 13 (March 1983): 788–92.

4. J. Iglehart, "Medicaid Turns to Prepaid Managed Care," *New England Journal of Medicine* 308, no. 16 (April 1983): 976–80.

5. Intergovernmental Health Policy Project, "Recent and Proposed Changes."

6. Iglehart, "Medicaid Turns to Prepaid," p. 976.

7. Ibid.

8. Intergovernmental Health Policy Project, "Recent and Proposed Changes."

9. Ibid.

10. Iglehart, "Medicaid Turns to Prepaid."

11. L. Bartlett, "Medicaid Freedom of Choice: A Review of Waiver Applications Submitted under Section 2175 of the Omnibus Reconciliation Act of 1981," The National Governor's Association, 1982.

12. Ibid., p. 2.

13. Ibid.

14. Iglehart, "Medicaid Turns to Prepaid," p. 978.

15. S. Sullivan, R. Gibson, P. Samors, J. A. Meyer, and R. McKinnon, "Restructuring Medicaid: A Survey of State and Local Initiatives," American Enterprise Institute Center for Health Policy Research, January 1983.

16. Ibid.

17. Ibid.

18. Bartlett, "Medicaid Freedom of Choice," p. 27–28.

19. Ibid.

20. Ibid.

21. Melia et al., "Competition," p. 788.

22. G. H. Ensign and J. J. Mayerhofer, "Medi-Cal Contracting: What Impact on California Hospitals?," *Hospital Progress* 64 (June 1983): 39.

23. Ibid.

2

The Historical Development of the Arizona Experiment

The Arizona Health Care Cost Containment System was enacted in November 1981, 15 years after the Social Security Amendments authorizing the Medicaid program were passed by the U.S. Congress. It has been calculated that $150 million dollars in federal tax revenues were lost to Arizona between 1967 and 1975 because of its failure to enact Medicaid legislation. Furthermore, it has been estimated that Arizona counties spent an additional $27,785,500 in fiscal year 1976–77 alone to provide health care for indigents who would have been eligible to use federal and state Medicaid funds.[1] There are a variety of political, economic, and social reasons for the unwillingness of Arizona legislators to participate in the Medicaid program and for the subsequent development of the AHCCCS legislation. In this chapter the historical background for the development of Arizona's county-based indigent health care delivery system is presented first, followed by a description of the legislative actions taken in Arizona in response to the passage of Medicaid. Then the chapter discusses the factors which led, ultimately, to the passage and implementation of AHCCCS.

The County-Based Indigent Medical Care System

Arizona county governments have been the traditional locus of responsibility for indigent medical care, with authority dating from 1864. Table 2.1 shows the legislative history of indigent health care in

Arizona, including the major actions taken by political leaders. In 1864, 48 years before Arizona became a state, the Howell Code was adopted, assigning to Arizona counties the full responsibility for the health care of the poor. Indigents were defined as those without jobs, or without relatives who could be required to provide funds for their medical care. Arizona Revised Statute 937, passed in 1887, gave the counties sole responsibility for provision of care. The responsibility of relatives was deleted, thereby increasing the responsibilities of counties.

Table 2.1 Legislative History of Indigent Health Care in Arizona

1864	Howell Code gave Arizona counties full responsibility for health care of indigents without jobs or relatives to provide for their care.
1887	ARS 973 passed. Statutory authority of counties as sole providers of indigent health care was established, and provision that indigents must rely on relatives for care or funds was deleted.
1901	ARS 11–297 was enacted in 1901 and remained in effect until 1981. Each of the 14 counties was given responsibility for the implementation of its own indigent health program, using at least the minimum eligibility standards set by the Arizona Department of Economic Security (DES).
1974	S.B. 1165 created the statutory basis for the implementation of a Medicaid program, beginning October 1, 1975.
1975	S.B. 1393 was passed to correct several problems in S.B. 1165. It deleted the medically needy from Arizona's Medicaid program, changed the mechanism used to calculate the level of county contributions, provided a procedure for county reimbursement of the state's Medicaid appropriation, and delayed implementation until July 1, 1976.
1975	A.Y. Young and Co. prepared a report on the expenditures of Arizona counties on indigent care, with projections allowing a calculation of actual costs incurred by each county. Released in January 1976, the cost calculation formula was not used by the Arizona legislature in its efforts to correct deficiencies in the Medicaid law, but directed attention on the outflow of tax funds to support Medicaid in other states.
1976	H.B. 2110 delayed implementation of Medicaid until August 15, 1977.
1977	Legislature and governor became aware of HEW provisions that allowed implementation of Medicaid on August 15, 1977, without further legislative change or appropriations from the state.
1977	House Resolution 2007 expressed the legislative intent regarding Medicaid: the legislature did not want Medicaid implemented without a state appropriation and considered illegal any attempts to do so.
1977	H.B. 2002 attempted to repeal the existing Medicaid statute, but was vetoed by the governor; an attempted senate override also failed. The

Continued

Table 2.1   Continued

justification for the attempted repeal was the belief that the Arizona Department of Health Services could implement the existing Medicaid statute, contrary to legislative wishes, without a state appropriation by requiring the counties to contribute funds.

1977   Fourteen Arizona counties petitioned the Arizona Supreme Court (May 31) to prohibit implementation of Medicaid by the Director of ADHS and asked for a determination of the legality of attempts to implement; Arizona Statewide Legal Services and Southern Arizona Legal Aid prepared an amicus curiae brief (June 10) giving the history, background and explanation of Medicaid and Arizona's involvement in the program.

The Arizona Supreme Court ruled (July 14) that the state Medicaid program was unconstitutional and could not be legally implemented under existing statutes. The director of ADHS was, therefore, prohibited from taking further action to implement Medicaid.

1978   H.B. 2002 unsuccessfully attempted to repeal the existing Medicaid statute, which the supreme court had found unconstitutional.

1978   H.B. 2403 was the vehicle for a senate amendment changing the county contribution formula to make the existing Medicaid statute constitutional. The attempt failed, leaving an unconstitutional Medicaid law on record.

1979   S.B. 1292, proposed by the governor, would have replaced the Medicaid statute with a health care program for children, using Medicaid funds. This effort failed to generate support at either the state or federal level.

1979   H.B. 2360 was a failed attempt to repeal the existing unconstitutional Medicaid statute and set up a study committee to consider the issues.

1980   H.B. 2307, proposed by the governor, would have created a state-funded alternative to Medicaid, with capitated services for AFDC recipients and foster care children. The effort failed.

1980   H.B. 2400 proposed to establish a state-funded alternative where counties could contract with the state to receive partial reimbursement for indigent health care. The goal was for counties to liberalize their eligibility standards and become involved in a prepaid, capitated program.

1981   A resolution of the County Supervisors Association of Arizona (March 5) called for a $15 million bailout and a permanent solution to the health care funding problem.

1981   S.B. 1007 became H.B. 2484, which passed the legislature and was vetoed by the governor; it was the precursor to the eventual AHCCCS law since it contained many of its important provisions.

1981   S.B. 1008, an emergency act, provided $5 million in aid to counties to provide health care for indigents.

1981   S.B. 1172 proposed amendments to the existing Medicaid statute to correct its constitutional deficiencies and add fraud controls and a

Continued

Table 2.1 Continued

	legislative oversight committee. It failed to pass.
1981	S.B. 1385, unsuccessful legislation proposed by the governor, would have created the "Arizona Health Service Delivery Act of 1981." The two main features of the proposal were: a pilot health assessment and screening program and a health care delivery system for AFDC recipients through prepaid, capitated plans, funded by the state as well as the counties.
1981	S.B. 1408 provided for state assumption of the county share of Medicaid through a capitated plan for the categorically needy and general assistance eligibles. The program would have required waivers from the federal government to receive Medicaid funds but did not pass.
1981	S.B. 1261, an attempted repeal of the existing Medicaid statute, again failed.
1981	H.B. 2475, termed the "county bailout," provided a formula to distribute $5 million to counties, as needed for indigent health care, in FY 1980–81. The bill, formerly S.B. 1008, was enacted.
1981	H.B. 2484, formerly S.B. 1007, was the immediate precursor to AHCCCS. It was passed by both the house and senate in the regular legislative session but was vetoed by the governor on April 25, 1981. The reason for the veto was the governor's belief that the law did not conform closely enough to federal Medicaid regulations to secure federal funding and that his signature would therefore be a "futile gesture."
1981	An initiative drive to appropriate funds for the state's Medicaid program did not collect enough signatures by the close of 1981 to put the issue on the ballot.
1981	Legislative leadership, staff, DHHS, HCFA, and White House representatives began discussions to arrive at waivers that could allow a demonstration program to begin.
1981	S.B. 1001, the Arizona Health Care Cost Containment System (AHCCCS), was enacted in a special legislative session and signed by the governor on November 18, 1981. It was a revision of H.B. 2484 and was approved by federal representatives as eligible to receive waivers and, therefore, federal Medicaid funds.

The role of Arizona counties in indigent health care was reaffirmed with the passage of A.R.S. 11–297 in 1901. This law assigned each of the 14 counties the task of implementing a medical care delivery system for indigents and further clarified eligibility standards. A.R.S. 11–297 assigned to the Arizona Department of Economic Security (DES) the responsibility for defining "indigency" as used by the counties in determining medical care eligibility. A set of minimum eligibility standards were determined by DES, and each county employed those standards, or more liberal ones, to determine eligibility for county-financed medical care. Net income and resources, including dwelling, automobile, and tools of trade, were used as the basis for eligibility determination. The basic provisions of A.R.S. 11–297 remained in effect for the next 80 years. In September 1981, prior to the passage of AHCCCS, there was wide variation in the income eligibility standards used by Arizona's counties: at one extreme, six counties employed the minimum DES standards while, at the other extreme, one county extended eligibility to individuals with incomes almost double that amount. (See table 2.2.) Calculations of coverage for dependents also varied between counties, making the requirements for participation quite different across the state.

Table 2.2   Income Eligibility Standards (September 1981)

County	Family Size[d]		
	1	2	3
Apache	$2,100	$2,800	$3,150
Cochise	2,100	2,800	3,150
Coconino	3,790	5,010	6,230
Gila	2,100	2,800	3,150
Graham[a]	2,100	2,800	3,150
Greenlee	2,800	3,700	4,450
Maricopa[b]	2,100	2,800	3,150
Mohave	3,360	4,500	5,640
Navajo	2,778	3,703	4,166
Pima	3,360	4,476	5,040
Pinal[b]	3,080[c]	3,896	4,285
Santa Cruz	2,100	2,800	3,150
Yavapai	3,420	4,500	4,860
Yuma	2,901	3,864	4,344
DES regulations	2,100	2,800	3,150

Source: Arizona Association of Counties survey conducted in September 1981.

[a] The standard is $2,460, $2,820 for two children, and $350 for each additional dependent.

[b] Other eligibility criteria are used for "part-pay" persons who receive a portion of services on a subsidized basis.

[c] For a single person over the age of 60, the standard is $3,381.

[d] Adjustments for additional dependents differ between counties and vary from a set dollar figure per dependent to different increments, depending on total number of dependents.

In addition, A.R.S. 11–297 provided the counties with considerable discretion in covered benefits, scope of services, and arrangements for delivery of those services. Table 2.3 shows the wide variation in services offered to indigents at no charge. While inpatient hospitalization, outpatient services, long-term care, pharmacy services, and emergency services were provided by all 14 counties, many other services were not provided everywhere, including prenatal care, well child preventive care (including immunizations), family planning, and eye examinations. A lack of uniform eligibility standards and county-by-county variation in scope of services caused problems for county and state program administrators. For example, counties with liberal benefits and eligibility levels tended to attract indigents with health problems. Also, efforts to devise a statewide system in the late 1970s were hindered by a lack of reliable data concerning the costs of providing a uniform level of care to the indigent population. As a result, estimates of the cost of delivering medical care to indigents in Arizona as constructed during development of the AHCCCS system were highly uncertain.

Arizona's Response to Medicaid

When the Medicaid legislation was passed in 1965 and implemented in 1967, the state of Arizona did not exercise its option to participate. While the state chose not to meet the initial 1970 participation deadline, the Arizona legislature did enact Senate Bill 1165 in May 1974.[2] This bill created the statutory basis for the implementation of Medicaid in Arizona on October 1, 1975. The bill specified that the nine federally mandated services would be covered and that both the mandatorily eligible (Aid to Families with Dependent Children, AFDC, and Supplemental Security Income, SSI) and the optional medically needy (those not eligible for the two categorical programs but still poor) would be included. County, rather than state, funds would be used to match federal dollars.

Three serious problems with S.B. 1165 were discovered after passage. First, the medically needy, defined by the federal government as those earning up to 133 percent of the AFDC income level, were not eligible for federal matching funds under the Arizona legislation. Thus, participation in Medicaid would be far more costly than the state had estimated if the medically needy were included. Second, due to the poor data provided by the 14 different county systems, it was impossible to determine the actual county expenditures on

Table 2.3 Services Offered to Indigents at No Charge

Categories	Counties[a]													
	1	2	3	4	5	6	7	8	9	10	11	12	13	14
Inpatient hospitalization	X	X	X	X	X	X	X	X	X	X	X	X	X	X
Prenatal care		X	X	X		X	X	X	X		X	X	X	X
Maternity services		X	X	X	X	X	X	X		X	X	X	X	X
Well child preventive care		X	X	X			X				X	X		
Childhood immunizations		X	X	X			X				X	X		
Outpatient services	X	X	X	X	X	X	X	X	X	X	X	X	X	X
Long-term institutional care	X	X	X	X	X	X	X	X	X	X	X	X	X	X
Home health care		X	X	X			X			X	X	X		X
Pharmacy services	X	X	X	X	X	X	X	X	X		X	X	X	X
Family planning services		X	X				X				X			X
Podiatry services	X	X		X				X	X	X	X	X	X	X
Dental screening services			X				X				X	X	X	
Restorative dentistry		X	X	X			X				X	X		X
Eye examinations		X	X	X	X		X			X	X	X	X	X
Eye examinations and glasses		X	X	X			X				X	X		X
Routine transportation		X			X		X					X		
Emergency transportation	X	X	X	X		X	X	X	X	X	X	X	X	X
Hearing aids											X			
Physical therapy	X	X	X	X	X		X	X	X	X	X	X	X	X

Source: Survey conducted by Arizona Association of Counties in September 1981 and personal conversations with county officials.

[a]
1 Apache	5 Graham	9 Navajo	13 Yavapai
2 Cochise	6 Greenlee	10 Pima	14 Yuma
3 Coconino	7 Maricopa	11 Pinal	
4 Gila	8 Mohave	12 Santa Cruz	

indigent health care necessary to establish county contribution levels. And finally, federal regulations required that at least 40 percent of the nonfederal dollars had to be state dollars, thereby negating one key aspect of the legislation: the use of county rather than state funds.

To correct these problems, the legislature passed S. B. 1393 in 1975. This deleted services for the medically needy, changed the county contribution from an expenditure basis to a formula basis, and required that the state be responsible for nonfederal dollars but that the counties reimburse the state for its expenditures. In addition, the new law delayed implementation until July 1, 1976. In the interim, doubts about the Medicaid program increased among Arizona policy makers, culminating in House Bill 2110 in 1976, which further delayed the implementation of Medicaid until August 15, 1977. During 1977, examination of the existing Medicaid statute raised the possibility that the program could be implemented without a legislative appropriation. That is, the director of the Arizona Department of Health Services (ADHS) could require that the 14 counties levy taxes and include in their annual budgets appropriations for the Medicaid program without any further legislative action. Therefore, the Arizona House passed Resolution 2007 expressing legislative opposition to implementation without an explicit appropriation by the legislature.

On May 31, 1977, the majority of Arizona counties sued the director of ADHS and other parties in response to a letter from the director requiring that they levy taxes and budget for participation in Medicaid. The counties petitioned the Supreme Court of Arizona to prohibit this action and asked for a determination of its legality, so that county budgets for the fiscal year beginning July 1, 1977 might be prepared with knowledge of any requirement for participation in Medicaid.[3]

The court granted permission for numerous legal aid, public legal services, religious, charitable, labor, and public social action organizations to file briefs amicus curiae in order to gain further input.[4] Estimates of the costs to the state of supporting Medicaid programs in the other 49 states, as well as the expenditure of funds by the counties for health care that would have otherwise been covered by the federal government, were offered in support of Medicaid participation. One brief suggested that if a portion of these existing county expenditures were utilized as the state share of a Medicaid program they would attract $38 million in additional federal funds, thereby assisting the counties in their efforts to provide indigent medical care.

In its decision, the court instructed the director of ADHS and remaining respondents to refrain from taking further action to implement the Medicaid program as it existed in Arizona law. Furthermore, the court determined that the Medicaid statute, as written, was unconstitutional and could not be implemented legally.[5] H.B. 2002 was introduced in January 1978 in an attempt to repeal the unconstitutional statute but failed due to lack of support in the senate. The senate next attempted to amend H.B. 2403 to correct those portions of the Medicaid statute that had been found unconstitutional, specifically addressing the formula that described the level of each county's contribution. This attempt failed when the house did not act on the senate amendments.

The governor of the state of Arizona became involved in the effort to establish a state-sponsored health care program for indigents when S.B. 1292 was introduced in February 1979. This bill was intended to replace the existing Medicaid statute with a health program for indigent children. The proposed program would use federal Medicaid and county funds to supply comprehensive health services, including a screening and prevention program, for eligible children. It met with little political support in Arizona, and federal officials declined to provide financial support. H.B. 2360, also introduced in 1979, again attempted to repeal the Medicaid statute as well as to establish a joint legislative study committee to "study the health care services available to the medically needy of this state and develop a plan for a comprehensive health care delivery system to meet the needs of the medically needy . . . and persons in this state other than the medically needy."[6] Once again, the legislature rejected the effort to repeal the flawed existing Medicaid statute.

In 1980, the governor proposed an alternative to Medicaid: a program for AFDC recipients and foster children using prepaid, capitated payments, funded totally by the state. Although this effort (H.B. 2307) failed, it set the precedent for a prepaid, capitated system. H.B. 2407, introduced in February 1980, proposed a system where counties would "contract with the state to receive partial state reimbursement for the promise of indigent health services. The rate of state reimbursement was designed to encourage counties to liberalize the minimum eligibility levels and participate in prepaid capitated programs."[7] This attempt also failed to gain enough legislative support for passage. Consequently, despite repeated efforts over a five-year period, public officials in Arizona had failed to either correct the consititutional deficiencies in the existing Medicaid statute, fund that statute, repeal it, or legislate an alternative. Beginning in 1980, economic and political events set the stage for a new, and ultimately successful, attempt to implement a statewide program for delivery of medical services to indigents.

The Enactment of the Arizona Health Care Cost Containment System

Inflation in the cost of providing health care for indigents in Arizona reached a critical level in the late 1970s. (See table 2.4.) Several rural counties reported that their costs had doubled between fiscal year 1978–79 and fiscal year 1979–80.[8] Furthermore, the average rate of increase across all counties for the same years was 26.9 percent. In the following year, extraordinarily large rates of increase were reported by Pinal County (86.1 percent), Navajo County (87.0 percent) and Apache County (77.4 percent), with many of the remaining rural counties also citing indigent health care budget increases of more than 50 percent during fiscal year 1980–81.

There were striking differences among counties in the reported average cost per client served, with the rural counties (12 of the 14 counties, excepting Pima and Maricopa Counties which include Tucson and Phoenix, respectively) facing costs per indigent of more than twice the levels in urban counties (see table 2.5). Furthermore, as shown in table 2.6, the relatively small "risk pool" of indigents in some of these counties made it difficult to budget for catastrophic illnesses. For instance, Santa Cruz County budgeted $942,576 for indigent care in fiscal year 1980–81 and spent $128,358 of this amount on four catastrophic illness episodes. Apache County spent $151,874 on three catastrophic illnesses out of a total indigent care budget of $524,948. The result of this overall inflation in health care costs, as well as expensive cases of catastrophic illness, was extreme pressure on county budgets.

In the past, it had been possible for the counties to raise sufficient revenue to meet unexpected indigent health care expenses and avoid overall budget deficits by increasing property tax rates. However, by fiscal year 1980–81, Arizona legislators were confronted with considerable constituent sentiment to enact a version of California's "Proposition 13." As a compromise, constitutional amendments were passed that imposed limits on the rate at which property

Table 2.4 Indigent Health Care Budget by County

County	1978–79	% Increase	1979–80	% Increase	1980–81[a]	% Increase[b]	1980–81[c]	1980–81 Overruns
Apache	$ 350,283	18.3	$ 414,309	26.7	$ 524,948	77.4	$ 734,910	$ 210,000
Cochise	3,972,105	3.0	4,085,052	18.7	4,848,439	36.8	5,588,439	740,000
Coconino	1,877,451	-15.5	1,587,042	25.8	1,996,317	38.4	2,196,317	200,000
Gila	2,537,290	.3	2,544,784	8.4	2,758,550	29.7	3,300,500	542,000
Graham	662,680	105.3	1,361,598	-10.0	1,225,429	-4.1	1,305,429	80,000
Greenlee	336,017	7.2	361,820	23.8	447,866	23.8	447,866	—
Maricopa	75,200,000	16.5	87,600,000	19.5	108,700,000	19.5	104,700,000	—
Mohave	2,052,607	-11.2	1,822,700	32.5	2,415,913	38.0	2,515,913	100,000
Navajo	530,853	7.3	570,421	87.0	1,066,771	87.0	1,056,771	—
Pima	23,000,377	60.0	44,224,735	4.4	46,155,481	5.9	46,855,461	700,000
Pinal	3,298,531	70.3	5,615,608	80.0	10,010,000	86.1	10,450,000	440,000
Santa Cruz	980,288	-7.1	843,794	11.7	942,576	99.5	1,682,143	739,560
Yavapai	1,806,868	45.8	2,634,330	5.8	2,786,525	19.1	3,136,969	350,440
Yuma	2,137,210	51.9	3,245,369	-7.6	3,000,000	7.9	3,750,000	750,000
Total	$118,742,560	32.1	$156,911,562	19.1	$186,878,815	22.2	$187,720,718	$4,852,000

Source: Arizona Association of Counties, April 2, 1981.

[a] Budgeted indigent health care expenditures in FY 1980–81.

[b] Increase from 1979–80 expenditures to budgeted expenditures plus overruns.

[c] Projected actual expenditures in FY 1980–81 as of 3/5/81, including budget overruns.

tax revenues could be increased (June 3, 1980). This left Arizona counties, and particularly rural counties, with few options in attempting to balance their budgets in the face of significant budget overruns for indigent medical care.

Proposed Legislative Solutions

In response to the growing fiscal pressures felt by Arizona counties, the state legislature passed H.B. 2475 (originally S.B. 1008). This bill, which became law, provided $5 million in supplemental state funds to "bail out" the counties for fiscal year 1980–81, according to a formula based on budget overruns in each county.[9] In addition, during the 1981 legislative session, 13 other bills were introduced addressing the health care problems of indigents (see table 2.1). Among these was H.B. 2484, a direct precursor to AHCCCS. This bill was passed in response to a March 5, 1981 meeting of the County Supervisors Association of Arizona. Representatives at this meeting called for emergency funding of $10 million for fiscal year 1980–81 to cover indigent health care deficits and for a permanent solution using county, state, and federal dollars.[10] H.B. 2484 was the only indigent health care bill passed during the regular 1981 legislative session. It allowed a $15 million supplement to county budgets for fiscal year 1981–82 and repealed the existing state Medicaid statutes, contingent on receipt of federal funds for an experimental program.

H.B. 2484 also contained the following features that were later included in the legislation that created the Arizona Health Care Cost Containment System: eligibility provisions including county, state, and small business employees as well as categorical eligibles and the medically needy; a specific formula for fiscal contributions by counties based on utilization; administration by a private contractor; competitive bidding by providers for contracts to provide prepaid care to eligibles; use of primary care gatekeepers; a specific set of benefits including emergency services; use of a Joint Legislative Health Care Cost Containment Committee to oversee programs; definition of penalties for fraud; and other specific eligibility and benefit features. While there was considerable controversy over H.B. 2484, it eventually passed both the house and senate. However, the governor vetoed the bill at the end of the legislative session (April 25, 1981) because he believed that one major goal of the bill—qualification for federal funds under Title XIX of the Social Security Act—would not

Table 2.5   County Costs Per Indigent Client (FY 1980–81)

County	County Cost	Clients Served	Average Cost Per Client Served
Apache	$ 542,883	227	$2,392
Cochise	3,422,997	2,616[a]	1,308
Coconino	1,652,304	1,830	903
Gila	1,579,790	1,847	855
Graham	767,538	1,331[a]	577
Greenlee	223,860	356	629
Maricopa	42,810,029	83,026	516
Mohave	1,915,737	1,104	1,735
Navajo	579,805	420	1,380
Pima	20,937,911	18,558	1,128
Pinal	5,468,145	5,500[a]	994
Santa Cruz	949,096	614	1,546
Yavapai	1,447,876	1,020	1,419
Yuma	3,276,965	2,543[a]	1,289
Arizona	$85,574,936	120,992	$ 707
Urban	$63,747,940	101,584	$ 628
Rural	$21,826,996	19,408	$1,390

Source: Arizona Association of Counties survey conducted in September 1981 and updated subsequently by Association staff.

Based on estimates by county government officials.

be achieved. His belief was based on the considerable variation between the proposed program and existing federal Medicaid regulations.

As a consequence of the governor's veto, the state Medicaid statutes were still law, and an initiative drive was undertaken by a number of advocacy groups to fund the program. The initiative proposed that "there is appropriated annually to the Arizona Department of Health Services from the State General Fund the sum of $48 million to meet the cost of the Statewide Medical assistance program."[11] The initiative drive did not accumulate sufficient signatures by the end of 1981 to force funding of Medicaid, but it did put additional pressure on legislators to resolve the indigent medical care dilemma in Arizona.

Adoption of AHCCCS: A Legislative Compromise

While the Arizona legislature now clearly desired to obtain federal funds to help pay for indigent medical care, influential conservative representatives, led by legislators from the Phoenix area, still resisted adoption of a traditional Medicaid approach for several reasons. First,

Table 2.6   Indigent Health Care Catastrophic Costs
(FY 1980–81)

County	No. Cases Over $10,000	Total Cost	Ave. Cost Per Case
Apache	3	$ 151,874	$50,625
Cochise[a]	35	1,100,000	31,429
Coconino	17	403,096	23,712
Gila	2	54,805	27,403
Graham	9	188,460	20,940
Greenlee	2	42,320	21,160
Maricopa[b]	475.5	8,568,209	17,982
Mohave	24	802,834	33,451
Navajo	7	147,916	21,131
Pima	60	1,200,334	20,006
Pinal	26	728,000	28,000
Santa Cruz	4	128,358	32,090
Yavapai	20	522,910	26,146
Yuma	35	839,137	23,975
Arizona	719.5	$14,878,253	$20,679

Source: Arizona Association of Counties.

[a] Estimated expenditures of $1.0 to $1.2 million for 30–40 cases.

[b] Estimated by county government officials.

they regarded Medicaid as poorly administered and lacking incentives for cost containment. Evidence for this viewpoint was based on substantial increases in Medicaid costs nationally since 1967, which these legislators blamed largely on its fee-for-service mode of financing. (Opponents of this viewpoint argued that the reasons for these cost increases included greater benefits, increases in the number of people served, increases in health care costs in general, and a disproportionate increase in the number of elderly, who required more services of greater intensity than the young.)[12] Their second criticism of Medicaid concerned the widely publicized instances of fraud and abuse of the program by both consumers and providers. Third, the conservatives claimed that the adoption of traditional Medicaid in Arizona would result in two separate indigent health programs, due to the prior existence of county-based systems, and that the uniformity of the Medicaid system nationwide would leave little opportunity for innovation in Arizona. Finally, legislative leaders in both the senate and house were very strongly federalist: they perceived the oversight, red tape, and bureaucracy that can accompany federal funds as particularly undesirable in Arizona. Therefore, for a variety of reasons, a traditional Medicaid program was still not acceptable to key Arizona legislators in the spring of 1981.

In spite of their antipathy towards a traditional Medicaid program, conservative legislators faced considerable pressure from various constituent groups to provide a viable alternative. The counties continued to demand fiscal relief, the initiative drive to fund the existing Medicaid statute remained a viable issue, business and industry leaders advocated the use of competition from the private sector and risk sharing by providers to help contain costs, and there were rumors of potential lawsuits based on the lack of uniform eligibility standards and benefits across the different county systems. As a result of these pressures, a legislative consensus gradually formed in support of four innovative features for an indigent medical care program: an expanded target group, including the medically needy and employed groups; involvement of the private sector in competitive bidding for contracts to deliver care; assignment of program administrative responsibility to a private firm selected in a separate competitive bidding process; and a set of cost containment measures, including the use of primary care gatekeepers and copayments.[13]

Because of this consensus and the governor's April 25 veto of H.B. 2484, the legislative leadership and staff, White House staff, and representatives of DHHS and HCFA began to discuss the possibility of receiving waivers from traditional Medicaid program requirements to initiate an indigent medical care "experiment." On September 19, 1981, the legislative leadership announced preliminary agreements on a series of waivers that would be provided to the state of Arizona by the federal government. Based on this agreement, the Arizona Health Care Cost Containment System was introduced and passed with bipartisan support on November 9 as S.B. 1001, in a special session of the Arizona legislature. The governor signed AHCCCS into law on November 18, 1981, creating a three-year demonstration project funded by the state, county, and federal governments under Title XIX of the Social Security Act.[14]

Summary

The Arizona Health Care Cost Containment System was enacted 15 years after the Medicaid program was implemented in the rest of the United States. The Arizona legislators accepted it because they believed it could avoid the cost inflation, fraud, and bureaucracy thought to be inherent in a traditional Medicaid program, and because legislative action was forced by powerful economic and political factors, including the potential bankruptcy of an existing county-based system of service delivery and pressure from industry to help contain health care costs by creating a "marketplace" environment featuring competition and prepayment. The result was an unusual and highly complex piece of legislation intended to be implemented in the ten-month period between its passage and a projected starting date of October 1, 1982. The actual provisions of S.B. 1001 are described in the next chapter. This description is followed in chapter 4 by a discussion of critical issues in the design of competitive bidding systems, particularly for indigent health care contracts.

Notes

1. Arizona Statewide Legal Services Project, Amici Curiae Brief, *Apache County et al.* v. *Suzanne Dandoy, M.D., et al.*, Supreme Court of the State of Arizona, June 10, 1977.
2. Arizona Association of Counties, Summary of the History and Status of the Provision of Indigent Health Care Services in Arizona, 1864–1980; 1981.
3. Petition for Special Action, *Apache County et al.* v. *Suzanne Dandoy, M.D., et al.*, Supreme Court of the State of Arizona, May 31, 1977.
4. Response to Petition for Special Action, *Cochise County et al.* v. *Suzanne Dandoy, M.D., et al.*, Supreme Court of the State of Arizona, July 14, 1977.
5. Arizona Association of Counties, Summary.
6. H.B. 2360, State of Arizona, 34th Legislature, 1st Regular Session, February 6, 1979.
7. Arizona Association of Counties, Summary.
8. Ibid. The existence of 14 different county-based indigent health care delivery systems prior to 1982 made it difficult for public officials to obtain reliable and comparable costs of delivering such care. The statistics presented in chapter 2 must, therefore, be viewed as approximate.
9. H.B. 2475, State of Arizona, 35th Legislature, 1st Regular Session, 1981.
10. Resolution, Supervisors Association's Request to the 35th Arizona State Legislature, March 5, 1981.
11. "An Initiative Measure," amending Title 36 A.R.S., adding section 36–2181, Number 3–I–82, 1981.
12. Arizona Statewide Legal Services Project, Amici Curiae Brief.
13. "Arizona's Proposed Health Care Cost Containment Approach," part of packet sent by Arizona Representative Burton S. Barr, House Majority Leader, to U.S. Congressman John Rhodes of Arizona, March 6, 1981.
14. Ibid.

3

The Legislation Creating
the Arizona Health Care
Cost Containment System

The legislation that created the Arizona Health Care Cost Containment System has been praised as highly innovative and capable of reshaping the delivery of medical services to indigents throughout the United States. In this chapter, the basic details of that legislation, particularly in regard to the competitive bidding process, are described. First, the cost containment features and administrative structure of the Arizona Health Care Cost Containment System are summarized, as they were defined in the legislation and accompanying documents. Next the competitive bidding process is outlined and pertinent features of the law that affect that process are described. Finally, the policy issues that were left to be resolved during implementation of the system are identified.

The Cost-Containment Features
and Administrative Structure
of AHCCCS

Although they are not explicitly listed as such in the legislation, AHCCCS contains seven mechanisms intended to contain program costs: primary physicians acting as gatekeepers; prepaid capitated financing; nominal cost sharing by consumers; limitations on freedom of choice of providers by consumers; capitated payment by HCFA to the state; competitive bidding to select a private firm as program administrator; and competitive bidding to select providers. The legislation also establishes an administrative structure to govern the program.

Primary Care Gatekeepers

Primary care gatekeepers, as defined in the law, include family and general practitioners, pediatricians, general internists, obstetricians, and gynecologists. Lawmakers intended that a statewide network of these physicians, who would act as "case managers," would serve to provide all general medical care as well as approval for the provision of all other types of care in order to reduce unnecessary and costly visits to specialists and emergency rooms. While cost containment was the explicit rationale behind the use of this mechanism, improved quality of care through better continuity of care and increased health maintenance and early detection activities also was claimed to be part of the legislative intent.[1]

Prepaid Capitated Financing

Prepaid capitated financing was intended to be the dominant mechanism by which providers would be reimbursed. The level of the reimbursement would be determined through a competitive bidding process conducted statewide, but with contracts awarded on a county-by-county basis. The use of "capped" fee-for-service payments would occur only when necessary, to cover service gaps most likely to occur in the rural counties, where countywide bids for all services might not be forthcoming. It was anticipated that cost containment would result from the lower hospitalization rates historically associated with prepaid health plans.[2]

Cost Sharing

Nominal cost sharing by enrollees was incorporated into the AHCCCS model in order to achieve three purposes, as outlined in the rules and regulations: "curtailment of overutilization; enhancement of patient dignity; and service utilization by members for truly needed health care."[3] The AHCCCS legislation specifies that rules and regulations be developed to require nominal copayments by all enrollees, except in emergencies, and possibly to require deductible, coinsurance, or premium payments by the medically needy population. In effect, the medically indigent and categorically eligible (AFDC and SSI) patients would be responsible for nominal copayments, while the medically needy would pay higher copayments and might be required to pay coinsurance representing a significant percent of costs. In no circumstance would a patient be denied service due to inability to share costs, and copayments would be waived in appropriate circumstances. It was intended that providers would collect the copayments and the program administrator or counties would collect co-insurance premiums from the medically needy. The actual mechanisms for collection of copayments and the amounts of the copayments were to be defined in the program's rules and regulations.

Freedom of Choice

Freedom of choice of providers is a requirement of traditional Medicaid programs but, as a research and demonstration project, AHCCCS received waivers from the federal government to allow limitations on free choice. It was expected that program enrollees would have a limited number of health plans, selected through the competitive bidding process, from which to choose. However, AHCCCS eligibles were to be offered a choice of those plan(s) available in their areas and were required to remain enrolled for at least a minimum time period, as defined by the AHCCCS director. The law also specified free choice of primary care physicians within contracting plans. Cost containment was expected because providers could more effectively manage service utilization by enrollees within their organizations than if all fee-for-service providers were available to program participants.

Sharing of Risk by the State

The state of Arizona was also expected to share the risk inherent in prepayment. Federal Title XIX funds would be available in an amount determined by the number of categorically eligible enrollees. It was estimated that 60 percent of the capitated rate for those enrollees would be prepaid to the state with adjustments made at the end of each year, as necessary to reflect differences between projected and actual enrollment.[4] It was intended that this arrangement would provide the state with an incentive to carefully monitor the costs and efficiency of AHCCCS.[5]

AHCCCS Administration Provided by Private Sector

A sixth feature of the program that was expected to contain costs relates more to the administrative structure of AHCCCS than to actions by providers and consumers. The AHCCCS director is required to "enter into an agreement with an independent contractor, subject to public bidding, to serve as the statewide administrator of the system. The Administrator has full operational responsibility, subject to the supervision by the director, for the system . . . "[6] The contract administrator was to be selected via a competitive bidding process early in the implementation phase of the program. The duties of the administrator, as outlined in the legislation, include contract administration and oversight of providers, implementation planning and operations in each county, technical assistance services to providers and potential providers, development of traditional accounting, MIS, and administrative functions, establishment of peer and utilization review processes, assistance in the formation of medical care consortia when needed in a county, and other management functions necessary to assure the provision of cost-efficient, high quality health care under AHCCCS. It was hoped that the managerial efficiency of the private sector would result in the provision of these services at a relatively low cost.

Competitive Bidding by Providers

Possibly the most innovative aspect of AHCCCS is the use of a competitive bidding process to develop contracts with organizations for comprehensive acute medical care. The AHCCCS legislation actually allows either "prepaid capitated health services contracts" or "discount advance payment contracts" with providers for a specified set of services. However, the former was favored as the mode of provider reimbursement, with the use of capped fee-for-service as an alternative in the event there were insufficient bidders to create a statewide network of prepaid providers. It was expected that bidders would use cost, population, and utilization data provided by the state in calculating their bids, and the law states that evaluation of both quality and price would be used in the bid award process. Competition among bidders for the right to deliver health care to indigents was expected to contain costs by restraining physician fees and hospital charges and by encouraging innovative, cost-conscious delivery methods.

Moreover, the inclusion of state, county, and employee groups in the AHCCCS program was expected to encourage HMOs and other health plans to compete for contracts. The competitive bidding feature of AHCCCS is the least clearly defined cost-containment strategy in the legislation, probably reflecting the technical nature of that process and, to some extent, the legislative expectation that existing state procurement rules would adequately define the bidding system.

Organizational Structure

Figure 3.1 presents a simple organizational chart depicting the relationships among the various entities involved in the AHCCCS program. The state AHCCCS Division directly supervises the AHCCCS administrator, with input from three sources: the Health Care Financing Administration (HCFA), within the U.S. Department of Health and Human Services (DHHS); the Arizona Department of Health Services (ADHS) and its director, within the executive branch of state government; and the Joint Legislative Health Care Cost Containment System Committee (called the Joint Legislative Oversight Committee, JLOC), mandated by the AHCCCS legislation and composed of "the chairmen of the House and Senate Health Committees as the co-chairmen, eight additional legislators as voting members, three county supervisors and the Directors of the Departments of Health Services and Administration as non-voting members."[7] The role of the JLOC is to assure that the legislative intent of AHCCCS is followed in the development of rules and regulations, to report to the legislators on the status of the program, and to provide a mechanism for health care providers to participate in the implementation process.

Legislative Framework for Competitive Bidding

The AHCCCS legislation defines only the basic requirements of the Arizona competitive bidding process. However, the literature identifies the following essential features of competitive bidding in general: a description of the qualifications of organizations eligible to bid; definition of the services to be included and excluded in each bid; description of the categories and potential numbers of recipients to be covered by each bid; identification of geographical areas covered by bids; the length of time that contracts will be in effect; the mechanics of bid submission; the criteria on which bids will be

Figure 3.1   Organizational Chart of Entities Involved in the Implementation of AHCCCS

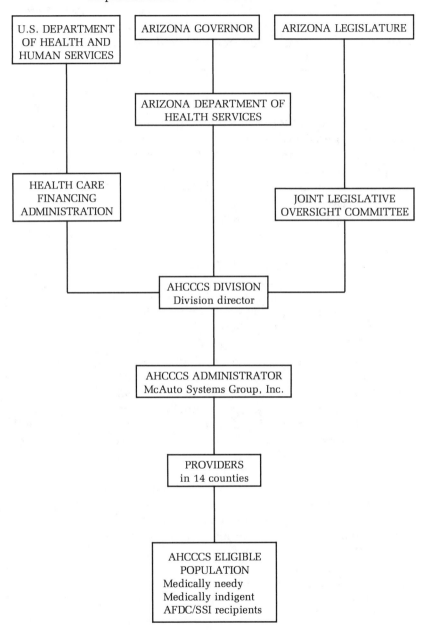

evaluated; the manner in which winning bidders will be reimbursed; and the contractual requirements of winning bidders. Each of these features is described in this section, both as explicitly defined in S. B. 1001 and as intended by policymakers, to the extent that those intentions can be discerned from public documents and interviews with program officials.

Potential Bidders

The legislation requires that a public invitation to bid be issued "to qualified group disability insurers, hospital and medical service corporations, health care service organizations (HMOs), and any other qualified public or private persons, including county owned and operated health care facilities,"[8] for the right to provide services to eligibles. Thus, the bid process was open to virtually any organization capable of providing, or arranging for, comprehensive or specific services (such as diagnostic tests, hospital care, transportation, etc.).

Categories of Eligible Populations

Under federal Medicaid requirements, several populations are mandatorily eligible for health care funded under Title III of the Social Security Act. These include recipients of Supplemental Security Income (SSI), including the poor aged, the blind, and the disabled. Any state using Title XIX funds must, therefore, cover Aid to Families with Dependent Children (AFDC) and SSI populations, although inclusion of two additional population categories is optional: the medically indigent (MI), the poor with personal income below $2,500 per year for single individuals and with net resources of $30,000 or less, as defined by the state of Arizona in S.B. 1001; and the medically needy (MN), the "near poor," with incomes between $2,500 and $3,200 per person and with net resources of $30,000 or less. The AHCCCS legislation adds a third set of potential participants to the program—Arizona state, county, and business employees and their eligible dependents. It was hoped that the participation of these individuals would increase the attractiveness of the program to potential bidders. Also, because providers would need to offer a desirable product to enroll the nonindigent participants, it was further hoped that their participation would improve the quality of services delivered to indigents by winning bidders.

The law establishes that all bidders must submit distinct bid prices for each of the following groups:

1. MI, AFDC, SSI, and MN
2. State employees (and dependents)
3. MI, AFDC, SSI, MN, and state employees (and dependents)
4. MI, AFDC, SSI, MN, and state and county employees (and dependents)
5. Business employees (and dependents)

In practice, although bids were submitted for these categories so that the program would be in technical compliance with the legislation, they were not utilized in the evaluation process. Instead, contract awards were based on additional bid prices submitted for the following categories: MN/MI, SSI-Blind, SSI-Disabled, SSI-Aged, and AFDC.

Service Categories

Arizona lawmakers were specific in their delineation of the services required for inclusion in each bid and the services that would not be covered by AHCCCS. The covered services are:

1. Inpatient hospital services including maternity care, but excluding institutional therapy for tuberculosis, mental disorders, and occupational and speech therapy for adults
2. Outpatient services provided in hospital, clinic, office, and other health care facilities by licensed providers under the direction of a physician, excluding occupational and speech therapy for adults
3. Laboratory and x-ray services
4. Medically necessary prescription medications
5. Emergency dental care and extractions
6. Medical supplies, equipment, and prostheses, excluding hearing aids
7. Treatment of medical conditions of the eye, excluding examinations and prescriptions for corrective lenses
8. Early and periodic health screening and diagnostic treatments (EPSDT) for children under 21, excluding eye examinations

for prescriptive lenses, nonorthodontic dental care, and hearing aids until October 1, 1983

The law also states that, with prior notification of providers, the department may modify, limit, or suspend mandatory services (under Title XIX) for the optional MN and MI populations and optional services for all populations if bids are above budgeted amounts or if at any time AHCCCS funding is insufficient to cover those services. An additional category of service required of bidders is transportation, including emergency ambulance and medically necessary transportation to and from providers. Furthermore, information and referral services must be made available to members regarding transportation, and counties are required to enroll eligibles in plans accessible by public transportation. Perhaps most importantly, long-term care of any type was excluded from AHCCCS, remaining the sole responsibility of the counties. Legislators felt that inclusion of long-term care would complicate and delay implementation of the program. However, they did state their intent to integrate long-term care into AHCCCS at some future date.

Service Areas

AHCCCS, as a replacement for a county-based health care delivery system, is oriented towards provision of services on a county-specific basis. Therefore, the law mandates that "the Director, in conjunction with the Administrator, shall prepare and issue a public invitation to bid in each of the fourteen counties of this state."[9] Services are required to be provided to enrollees in their county of residence, with certain exceptions: emergency services, specialty services if authorized by the member's primary care physician, and health and medical services "if a net reduction in transportation costs is achieved."[10]

Length of Contracts

Lawmakers were apparently reluctant to make a policy decision about the term of contracts with winning bidders, since any length chosen could be construed as favoring either providers or the state. Therefore, the choice of a contract length was left to program administrators, provided that they would ask for bids "at least once every two years."[11]

Bid Process

Only basic guidance in the mechanics of the competitive bidding process is provided in the AHCCCS legislation. Lawmakers stipulated that a public invitation to bid, including a proposed contract format, be issued to all eligible bidders, with bids to be submitted for the services and populations listed above. Further conceptualization of the process was to be contained in the program rules and regulations. The law does require "the awarding of contracts to providers with the lowest qualified bids."[12] The term "qualified" was not defined, leaving public officials with little guidance as to legislative intent in this regard. Also, the meaning of "lowest" was not explained, creating uncertainty as to the number of contracts that would be awarded in each county. The legislation left open the possibility that multiple contracts for specific geographic areas could be executed.

Evaluation of Bids

Evaluation of bids is barely addressed in the AHCCCS legislation, except for several allusions to evaluation schemes to be defined in program rules and regulations. It was suggested that evaluators would be allowed to adjust the four basic service categories (inpatient, outpatient, pharmacy, and laboratory, x-ray, and related diagnostic medical services and appliances) "by expansion, deletion, segregation, or combination in order to secure the most financially advantageous bids for the system."[13] Analysis of all of the bids in each county on an aggregate basis is also permitted in order to guarantee the provision of all types of required services throughout each county. The five bid prices to be submitted by each bidder, based on separate and combined groups of eligible populations defined in the legislation, were intended to be used to help policymakers evaluate the relative costliness of each bid to the state and counties. (Termed the "legislative compliance" groups, these five categories were not actually used in bid evaluation.) In summary, with the exception of the provision that the "lowest qualified" bidders in each county be awarded contracts, Arizona lawmakers left the technical aspects of the evaluation of bids to be developed during the implementation period.

Contractual Requirements

In addition to requirements specifying the services to be provided by plans, the law also includes other conditions of contract compliance relating to the availability of records for inspection by the AHCCCS director and administrator, as well as the U.S. Department of Health and Human Services. A third set of conditions relates to the need for assurance of adequate performance by the providers according to their contracts. "Performance" relates to the risk, inherent in a prepaid health care delivery system, that providers might fail financially. Therefore, Arizona policymakers created latitude for the director to require providers to maintain financial deposits, performance bonds, financial reserves, or other means of ensuring either adequate performance or coverage of care in the event of default. Furthermore, the director was given the power to retain a specified portion of each monthly or quarterly payment to providers. These funds would establish a reserve that could be used to provide financial incentives to maintain quality care and minimize unnecessary hospitalizations according to performance standards set by the director.[14] No guidance was provided in the legislation concerning how financial incentives could be designed to accomplish these objectives.

Policy Issues Not Addressed by Legislation

There are a variety of explanations for the relative lack of specificity in the AHCCCS legislation with regard to the competitive bidding system, as well as the program in general. These include unwillingness of elected officials to make explicit, and potentially unpopular, political decisions; lack of knowledge concerning the technical aspects of administering a prepaid health care delivery system based on contracts; concern about unwittingly discouraging the level of participation of providers and HMOs in the program; and, finally, the need for rapid passage of the legislation in an already crowded special legislative session.

The major questions relating to competitive bidding that were left to be answered in the implementation phase included:

— Would single contracts be awarded, or would multiple providers be chosen so as to provide some freedom of choice for enrollees and protection for the state in the event of financial failure or withdrawal of providers?

— What criteria, besides price, would be used to evaluate the bids submitted by prospective providers?

— What would public officials do if the price of the bids, when multiplied by the number of potential enrollees, exceeded the AHCCCS program budget?

— How would officials deal with existing county delivery systems maintained by the two highly populated urban counties and many of the more rural counties in the event they were not chosen as winning bidders?

— Should AHCCCS officials explore different reimbursement mechanisms, or should they simply reimburse providers at the level of their bids?

— How long should contracts with providers be in effect? Should renewal through negotiation be permitted?

— Should plans offering all health services be favored in the evaluation process over providers proposing to contract for only one specific service? Should the administrator attempt the time-consuming and costly process of developing health service delivery networks from partial service bids?

Summary

While highly innovative in its approach to cost containment in the delivery of medical services to indigents, the AHCCCS legislation provided only the basic structure for implementation of the program. The law was particularly vague on how the competitive bidding process for the selection of providers would be designed and managed. Rules governing the operation of the bidding process, criteria to be used for the award of contracts, the length of time contracts would be in effect, groupings of indigents to be covered by bids, and the impact of a fixed budget on the award process were all left to be developed during implementation of the program. The reasons behind the lack of definition of these processes are unclear, but probably indicate lack of technical expertise, time constraints, and imperatives to develop an indigent health care delivery system that would be politically acceptable.

Notes

1. Personal communication, Arizona State Senator Carl Kunasek.
2. AHCCCS Rules and Regulations, Preamble, May 27, 1982.
3. Ibid.
4. Legislative Interpretation of S.B. 1001, November 9, 1981.
5. AHCCCS Rules and Regulations, Preamble.
6. S.B. 1001, State of Arizona, 35th Legislature, 4th Special Session, 1981, p. 11.
7. Summary of Legislative Provisions—AHCCCS, November 9, 1981.
8. S.B. 1001.

9. Ibid., p. 16, Section 362906B.
10. Ibid., pp. 18–20, Section 362907.
11. Ibid., p. 16, Section 362906B.
12. Ibid., p. 17, Section 362906C7.
13. Ibid., p. 17, Section 362906C.
14. Ibid., p. 14.

4

Issues in the Design of Competitive Bidding Systems for Indigent Contracts

The Arizona Health Care Cost Containment legislation described in the previous chapter, while vague with respect to specific design features, suggests a competitive bidding process for indigent patients that is a natural extension of the straightforward bidding processes commonly employed in state procurement situations. These bidding processes generally consist of four steps. First, the state defines the rules governing the operation of the bidding system. Second, qualified organizations are invited to submit bids. Third, winners of the bidding competition are selected on the basis of criteria known by participants prior to bid submission. Finally, contracts with winning bidders are established and enforced to ensure that the state receives value in return for the dollars it expends. As chapter 3 points out, however, the legislation provided little guidance with respect to the first step, the bidding system design, leaving its features to be specified in the program's implementation phase.

In this chapter, we discuss the incentives inherent in the bidding system implied by the legislation. In some cases, we discuss other approaches that the state might have adopted. We pay the greatest

This chapter was previously published in the Winter 1984–1985 issue of *Contemporary Policy Issues*, a journal of the Western Economics Association. Reprinted with permission of the journal of *Contemporary Policy Issues*.

attention to alternate methods that the state might have considered in reimbursing providers under competitive bidding and the implications of these mechanisms for program costs. We also address several related design issues, some of which were not clearly identified in the legislation. These issues include the length of the contract awarded, the grouping of indigents for contract awards, the use of reservation prices and negotiation by the state, and the determination of system capacity. The chapter concludes with a discussion of the politics of competitive bidding system design and its likely effect on different design choices.

Reimbursement Rules and Program Costs

From the point of view of state officials, a major objective in the design of competitive bidding systems for indigent medical care is the identification of bidding rules that minimize program costs. Program costs are directly related to the levels of the bids submitted by providers and the procedures used to determine reimbursement levels for winning organizations. In his seminal paper, Vickrey (1961) first pointed out that the level of an auction bid price depends in part on the reimbursement rule announced by the seller prior to the submission of bids.[1] The voluminous literature pertaining to competitive bidding in general identifies a variety of different reimbursement rules that states might adopt in their indigent medical care programs.[2] The discussion that follows is focused on two variations of a "sealed bid" auction and one type of "oral" auction. A sealed bid auction is a bidding process in which bid prices are secret until all bids have been submitted. An "oral auction," as the name implies, features some form of price disclosure during the auction process.

Comparing Sealed Bid Auction Alternatives

The procedure ultimately adopted in the AHCCCS program, although not precisely specified in the legislation, involved reimbursement of all winning bidders at the rates specified in their bids. In the bidding literature this is referred to as a "discriminative" or "first price" sealed bid auction. When employed in indigent medical care programs, it results in the payment of different prices for the same medical services if multiple bidders are selected as "winners." Also, providers who believe that they have lower costs than their competitors have an incentive to "out-guess" the process by submitting bids that exceed their true costs. In this way they can secure some reward for their efficiency. However, if they overestimate their comparative efficiency they run the risk of not being selected as a winning bidder. This risk increases with the number of potential competitors. Consequently, in a discriminative auction, providers are rewarded both for their cost effectiveness and for their ability to successfully "game" the system in submitting bids.

A second commonly discussed option for sealed bidding systems is the reimbursement of all winning bidders at the level of (or marginally above) the highest winning bid, or at the lowest excluded bid if only one winner is chosen. This type of auction has been labeled a "competitive," "second price," or Vickrey sealed bid auction. It results in the payment of a single price for the defined set of services if multiple bidding organizations are awarded contracts. Under the competitive auction there is little incentive for low cost bidders to "pad" their bids; padding does not enhance their profits if they are selected but increases the risk of not being selected. Therefore, under most variations of this auction, providers have strong incentives simply to submit bids that most accurately reflect their estimated costs of delivering the specified services.[3]

On the surface it would appear that the competitive auction would result in greater program costs for the state. This is not necessarily true, however, as was brought out in an interesting exchange between Andrew Brimmer (1962) and Milton Friedman (1963) over the proper design of Treasury Bill auctions.[4] Since there is an incentive under discriminative rules for bidders to submit prices higher than their true costs, it is likely that all, or most, of the bids received in a discriminative auction will be higher than under competitive auction rules. This situation is illustrated in figure 4.1 for a hypothetical bidding process involving indigent medical care, with bidding organizations designated by A–E. Bids under each option are arranged along the horizontal axis in ascending order of price. The graph is drawn to illustrate a situation where the bids submitted by each organization under discriminative rules exceed their corresponding bids under competitive rules because of gaming behavior. If a capacity to provide care to 50,000 indigents is desired, and all bidders are judged to be acceptable on all other criteria, bidders A and B would be selected.

Because of the incentive to pad bids under discriminative rules, it is possible that total program costs to the state under this option would exceed the expenditures required to reimburse both A and B

Figure 4.1   Hypothetical Bid Levels under Two Reimbursement
Alternatives

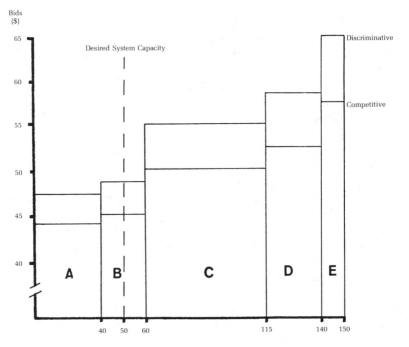

Bids
($)

Desired System Capacity

Discriminative

Competitive

A   B   C   D   E

40   50   60   115   140   150

Potential System Capacity (thousands of eligibles)

at B's bid price, assuming all providers knew prior to bidding that winners would be reimbursed at the highest winning bid. Figure 4.2 illustrates that this is the case under the circumstances depicted in figure 4.1. Total annual expenditures under the discriminative rules ($2.37 million) exceed those required under the competitive rules ($2.25 million) by the shaded amount. Of course, it is also possible that the discriminative auction could be less expensive for the state than the competitive auction. For example, in figure 4.3 the increase in profit enjoyed by bidder A ($40,000), when both A and B receive the same reimbursement under the competitive auction ($48), exceeds the amount that bidder B would receive in excess of true costs ($y = \$10,000$) under discriminative auction rules. (For expositional purposes, it is assumed that all organizations bid the same capacity under each set of rules and the state assigns eligibles to the lowest cost plan if they do not make a choice among plans.)

Figure 4.2   Total Cost of Reimbursement in Discriminative Auction
Exceeds Cost of Competitive Auction

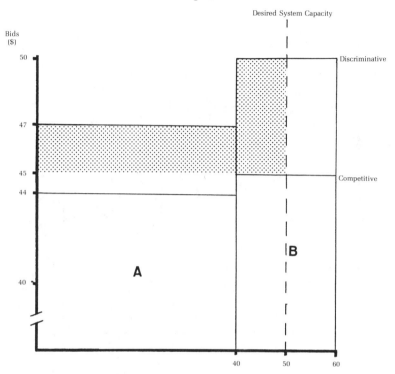

Capacity of Bidders A and B (thousands of eligibles)

Since the Brimmer/Friedman exchange, a number of authors
have attempted to define the conditions under which competitive auction revenues would exceed discriminative revenues, or vice versa,
in auctions where the highest sealed bid determines the winner(s).
Although these authors have investigated auctions that do not per-
fectly reflect the institutional characteristics of bidding processes for
indigent medical care, and their assumptions and approaches often
vary, their results do provide some insight into the behavioral implications of the two sets of rules.[5]

Several authors have addressed the question by developing
mathematical models based on rigorously defined auction rules and
rather strict assumptions about bidder behavior. For example, Riley
and Samuelson (1981) assume that each bidding group is uncertain

Figure 4.3   Total Cost of Reimbursement in Competitive Auction
Exceeds Cost of Discriminative Auction

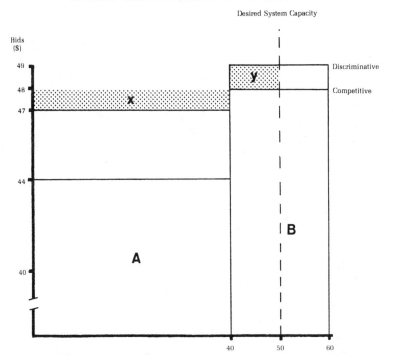

Capacity of Bidders A and B (thousands of eligibles)

about the value that other bidders attach to the item being auctioned
and that bidders decide the maximum amount they are willing to pay
independently of other bidders. In addition, all bidders share common
beliefs about the possible estimates held by others. The result is that
estimates of bidders are independent, identically distributed, and
drawn from a common distribution.[6] If all bidders are risk neutral and
pursue optimal bidding strategies, Riley and Samuelson (1981) show
that revenue is the same under both auctions. However, under the
assumption that bidders are risk averse, more revenue is generated
by the discriminative auction. Riley and Samuelson (1981)
acknowledge that the basic assumption of value independence is not
tenable in most real world situations, where "a good's economic value
to a potential buyer consists of two parts—a value element which is
common to all market participants and one which is buyer specific."[7]

This clearly is a more appropriate description of the environment in which bidding on indigent medical care takes place.

Ramsey (1980) addresses the revenue-generating properties of the two auctions at some length in his theoretical analysis of bidding for offshore oil leases. He assumes that a single object is auctioned, each bidder has the same access to information as every other bidder, and bidders react to the aggregate behavior of competitors but not the individual actions of specific competitors. Within this framework, he proves that any organization's optimal bid under discriminative bidding rules will be less than under competitive bidding. More importantly, he finds that, in short-run equilibrium, discriminative auction bidding rules result in greater revenue if bidders are nearly risk neutral, have large wealth, and are few in number. But competitive rules generate more revenue if bidders are highly risk averse, have limited wealth, and are great in number.[8]

The results of Ramsey (1980) differ from those of Riley and Samuelson (1981) and seem to be based on a model with behavioral assumptions and institutional constraints more closely reflecting the bidding process for indigent medical care. However, even if his conclusions were comparable for the case where the right to deliver services is awarded to the low bidder, they would not settle the issue of which set of bidding rules, when applied to indigent medical care programs, would result in the lowest costs for the state. Participants in an indigent medical care bidding process are likely to be relatively few in number, suggesting that a discriminative auction would be preferable based on Ramsey's results. However, they may be highly risk averse and have limited wealth, which would argue that competitive auction rules should be adopted.

A second approach to analyzing the potential costs to the state of the two auctions relies on carefully structured experiments, where parameters of interest are systematically varied. Smith (1967) conducted experiments where participants submitted sealed bids specifying both quantity and price. He found that revenues to the seller are greater in a competitive auction than in a discriminative auction when the proportion of rejected bids is low or moderate but that this conclusion does not hold when the number of rejected bids is high.[9]

Miller and Plott (1983) devised a series of experiments directed at comparing the revenues of each auction to the seller under different assumptions about buyer price elasticity of demand. They conclude that discriminative auctions generate more revenue for the state if demand curves are steep, but competitive auctions are preferable if demand curves are flat. These results did not always hold during the initial rounds of bidding in the experiment, since the bids in the discriminative auctions showed substantial variability.[10] Miller and Plott (1983) also speculate that if risk aversion is present among bidders, then increasing the number of bidders relative to a fixed quantity of items to be auctioned could result in a steeper demand curve. This would make the discriminative auction more attractive for the state. If similar behavior to that observed in the Miller and Plott (1983) experiments held in indigent medical care auctions where the bids generate a supply curve and an award is made to the lowest bidder, then discriminative auctions would result in lower program costs for steeper supply schedules, while competitive auctions would be preferable if supply schedules were fairly flat.

This brief review of the literature suggests that generalizations concerning the relative costs of discriminative versus competitive auction rules for bidding on indigent medical care are difficult to support based on existing research. The major research efforts to date have concentrated on auctions where awards are made to the highest bidder, in contrast to the low bidder criterion used in awarding indigent medical care contracts. In addition, mathematical modeling has focused on institutional settings (e.g., offshore oil) with characteristics that differ from indigent medical care auctions and has required rather severe assumptions about bidder behavior to achieve definitive outcomes. Experimental methods seem promising as a means of addressing the question, but no studies to date have captured important characteristics of the bidding process for indigent medical care.

There are several possible variations on these two sealed bid reimbursement rules that may be attractive to state policymakers, but whose consequences have not been fully explored in the published literature. For instance, a hybrid of the discriminative and competitive auctions could be constructed, in which bidders are reimbursed the amount of their bids plus some fraction of the difference between their bids and the highest winning bid. Depending on the level at which the "fraction" is set and the characteristics of the bidders, the incentives for developing cost-containing innovations could be weaker than in a pure competitive auction, since the financial return for submitting a low bid would be less. There would be some strategic behavior, but possibly less than under discriminative rules.

In a second variation, a portion of provider profits could be distributed to patients by permitting winning bidders to voluntarily add benefits to the list of required services on which bidding was based. By adding benefits, low bidders presumably would attract more patients if patients were given a choice of plans at enrollment, achieve capacity enrollment sooner, and therefore have lower average administrative costs per patient. A variation of this idea would permit winning bidders in a competitive auction to offer additional benefits in dollar form. For example, providers could institute savings accounts for enrollees in their plan. These accounts would grow with a fixed monthly contribution by providers, and enrollees could draw on them as necessary to cover any copayments that might be required for services. (While copayments are now minimal under the AHCCCS and most indigent medical care programs, they could grow in popularity in the future as a means of restraining utilization and consequently state program costs.) At the end of each year, enrollees could be remitted all, or a portion, of the amount remaining in the accounts. The "savings account" would create incentives for patients to use care wisely, while at the same time lowering any financial barriers to essential care that might be created by the presence of even minimal copayments. It also would provide another opportunity for low bidders to exploit their cost-effectiveness to attract enrollees.

The Ascending Dutch Auction

While discriminative and competitive auctions using sealed bids have received the bulk of the attention in the bidding literature, variations on these auction rules may be attractive to the state for political reasons. For instance, there may be political pressures on state officials to adopt bidding procedures that give the appearance of greater direct control over program expenditures. Under sealed bid discriminative and competitive rules, program costs cannot be determined exactly in advance; they are in effect determined by the bid levels of providers. Therefore, these bidding systems are somewhat at odds with political desire to "gain control" over entitlement programs by converting them into fixed budget items.

The ascending Dutch auction, a competitive bidding system, has the political virtues of permitting the state administrators to appear to exert direct control over program expenditures. In the Dutch auction (named after its use in the flower markets of the Netherlands), the state announces a reimbursement level per enrollee per month and then invites any qualified group of providers to participate at that price. The initial announced reimbursement level could be based on the budgeted funds available for the projected number of enrollees or could begin below this amount. If the initial announced price does not achieve the desired system capacity, the state can raise the price by a specified amount until this capacity is attained. If providers are paid the per enrollee per month prices at which each commits to provide services (the discriminative rule), then a provider who successfully pledges to serve N individuals at one price and Q more at a higher price would be paid the lower price for the first N and the higher price for the next Q enrollees. Alternatively, every successful bidder could be paid an amount for each individual served equal to that price at which desired system capacity is finally reached. In this case, all winning bidders would be reimbursed at the same amount, equal to the highest accepted price, a procedure consistent with competitive reimbursement rules.

The bidding literature has devoted considerably more attention to investigating the properties of sealed bid auctions than to analyzing Dutch auctions of the type just described. Vickrey (1961) has characterized the Dutch auction as a "game" in which each bidder needs to take into account information about probable bids by others, while bids by others depend in part on expectations about the bidder's own behavior.[11] In this situation, the submission of a bid equal to the estimated value of providing care would maximize the likelihood of being awarded the contract but would result in no profit if discriminative reimbursement rules were followed. However, the longer the bidder waits in the ascending Dutch auction, the greater the risk of not winning.

It is clear that the Dutch auction contains some of the same motivations for strategic behavior as the sealed bid discriminative auction. Cox, Roberson, and Smith (1982) performed a series of experiments comparing the descending Dutch auction (the seller begins at a high level and then systematically reduces the price) to sealed bid discriminative and competitive auctions where the highest bid wins. They found that the Dutch auction, where reimbursement is at the bid price, elicits more strategic gaming by bidders and therefore lower bids than the sealed bid discriminative auction.[12] If a similar result were obtained in an ascending Dutch auction for indigent medical care, then the state would ultimately have higher program costs under the Dutch format than under sealed bid discriminative rules. The relationship between program costs under the Dutch and sealed bid competitive formats is not clear.

The political attractiveness of the Dutch auction relative to either sealed bid alternative results from the proactive role the state can play in the bidding process. In appearance, the state can exert greater control over providers by determining the level of the initial price announcement and the increments and timing of the subsequent price increases. In this sense, the Dutch auction represents a public, formalized, although one-sided, negotiation process.

Related System Design Issues

While the definition of reimbursement rules for providers plays a key role in the design of any competitive bidding process, there are several other issues relating to bidding system design that state policymakers must also address. Some have not been analyzed in the bidding literature, while limited research applies to others. Several of these additional issues are introduced briefly below.

Contract Length and Market Entry

In bidding processes that result in long-term contracts for the winning bidders, the contractual obligations are often not defined precisely at the time of bid submission. This permits negotiation between the state and winning bidders if unforeseen developments occur, but introduces a number of problems in contract administration relating to the potential "capture" of program officials by contract awardees.[13] Short-term contracts, as adopted by the AHCCCS, can be used to avoid some of these hazards: "Indeed, recognizing that a bidding competition will be held in the near future, winning bidders may be more inclined to cooperate with the franchising authority, if specific contractual deficiencies are noted, rather than use such occasions to realize temporary bargaining advantages."[14] However, even in a bidding system featuring short-term contracts, the incumbent may have advantages in rebidding. Presumably winning bidders will accumulate considerable information on which to base future bids and will naturally be reluctant to make all of this information public. Through their ongoing relationships with program administrators, contract awardees may be able to influence bidding rules in their favor. Finally, previous winners can call for special consideration in the awarding of contracts based on the desirability of providing continuity of care for program participants. To the extent that incumbent bidders do have an unnatural advantage in bidding, the cost-containment potential of the competitive bidding process is compromised. Incumbent organizations that do not face the real possibility of nonrenewal have weaker incentives for efficiency in service delivery and stronger incentives to pad their bids under discriminative auction rules.

Composite Prices and the Awarding
of Contracts

In AHCCCS, although participants in the bidding process submitted separate bids for each of five categories of indigent eligibles, an artificial composite bid price was used in selecting winning bidders (see chapter 5). The selection of different winning providers for each eligible group was rejected by AHCCCS officials in the first round of bidding, partly because it was feared that providers might "skim the cream" by bidding on groups characterized by low utilization (e.g., AFDC) while ignoring groups with high utilization (e.g., SSI). Also, it was felt that established providers might believe the inclusion of the medically indigent in their patient population would reduce their ability to enroll members of private employed groups (see chapter 7). Therefore, provider bids on the "less desirable" groups might be higher to take into account this potential indirect cost.

It seems unlikely that high utilizing groups would be ignored in a competitive bidding process, since all bids would incorporate estimates of utilization and providers could potentially profit from a contract to serve any group. Furthermore, the awarding of separate contracts for each group would be one way of creating an additional capacity for expansion within the system. If a winning provider for one group of eligibles faced financial difficulties, providers serving different groups could be permitted to expand their patient populations. This could provide "back up" capacity in the system to be used in the event of the economic failure or inadequate performance of a provider, without incurring the additional costs of selecting winning bidders based on composite prices.

Rassenti, Smith, and Bulfin (1982) have devised a method for awarding contracts where bids on multiple items are submitted simultaneously and where bidders can specify contingencies as part of their bids.[15] For instance, a bidder might wish to limit the number of SSI eligibles who can be enrolled at the bid price, but place no such constraint on other categories of eligibles. Their method appears to be applicable to bidding on indigent medical care and could provide a mechanism for minimizing costs while also responding to other objectives of both bidders and program officials.

Reservation Prices and Negotiation

A reservation price is that value determined by the state prior to an auction as the "cutoff" level for bids. In bidding for construction contracts, the "engineers' estimate" is sometimes used as a benchmark for acceptable bids,[16] while geological estimates are used to calculate lower bounds for bids on offshore oil leases.[17] The state's reservation price may be kept secret until after the submission of bids, or it may be revealed during the bidding process. Under the assumptions of their model, Riley and Samuelson (1981) prove that, when numerous bidders are competing, the bidding process would not be jeopardized by publication of the reservation price prior to the submission of bids.[18] The intuition behind their result is clearest for the competitive sealed bid auction, where the dominant strategy for bidders is generally to submit a bid reflecting their best possible estimate of the costs of providing care irrespective of other information.

Smiley (1979) investigates the use of reservation prices in some detail, employing a mathematical model of discriminative auctions for offshore oil where there is one winning bidder for each lease tract. He concludes that announcing the reservation price can reduce bidder uncertainty, increase the competitiveness of the auction, and increase the level of bids. The use of a reservation price protects the state against the possibility that all bidders might underestimate the true value (or overestimate the cost) of the item being auctioned.[19] Brown (1969) also points out that reservation prices in the presence of capital constraints can provide "protection against those who would enter low bids without expecting to win many objects, but hoping for large net returns . . . on those few objects purchased."[20]

In auctions for indigent medical care, a reservation price could be based on the budgeted funds available for the projected number of enrollees or, alternatively, on the estimated cost per indigent of providing care through the most likely alternative—the fee-for-service medical care system. If all bids exceeded its reservation price, the state could take one of three actions: ask for rebids, reimburse for care under the fee-for-service system, or negotiate with providers. None of these alternatives is attractive as a means of system reform. There is no guarantee that lower bids would result from rebidding. In fact, if competitive auction rules were employed previously, theory predicts that providers would submit essentially the same bids in the second round unless the "information content" of the revealed reservation price was judged sufficient by bidders to lead them to reevaluate their costs. Meanwhile, delays caused by rebidding could result in a gap in access to care for program enrollees. The high costs associated with the fee-for-service system presumably provided some of the motivation for instituting competitive bidding, and therefore reversion to fee-for-service would not be an attractive alternative for program administrators. This leaves the possibility of negotiating with bidders. While it can be effective the first time it is employed, negotiation creates perverse incentives for subsequent rounds of bidding. If providers learn to anticipate negotiation over bids, they can protect their positions by padding their bids, incorporating something to "give up" in the negotiation process.

System Capacity

A primary goal of state officials is to develop sufficient capability through the competitive bidding process to serve at least the number of eligibles expected to enroll in the program. When bidders can specify limits on the number of eligibles they will serve, the selection of more than one winning bidder may be necessary, and this may generate system capacity that exceeds enrollment projections. There are several reasons why the state may feel it is desirable for the capacity of the system to exceed the projected number of eligible indigents in a given area.

First, the concept of consumer choice might be supported on philosophical grounds. Excess system capacity could provide at least some consumers with a choice among winning provider groups at the time of enrollment. They could exercise their preferences with respect to provider location and reputation, even though there would be no differences in price or basic benefit package among the winning provider groups. If winning providers are allowed to compete for patients by adding to the required benefit package, as discussed above, patients presumably would have stronger incentives to evaluate their enrollment options.

A second justification for excess capacity is its value as a hedge against the adverse consequences of the financial collapse of a winning provider group. The financial collapse of a provider is more likely under discriminative rules, unless all winning bidders have correctly assessed their relative costs and padded their bids accordingly. Under competitive auction rules all winning providers but one are reimbursed at more than their bids, providing a financial cushion for most providers. The possibility of a financial collapse, and hence the importance of maintaining excess capacity to guard against it, should decrease with each round of bidding as more information is generated concerning the utilization levels of the different groups of program eligibles and more experience is gained in managing the provider organizations.

The final justification for maintaining excess capacity is perhaps the most compelling—it could make the enforcement of contracts easier for the state. Program officials would be more likely to terminate a contract for inferior performance if alternative capacity were already in place to service some or all of the program participants enrolled with that provider. Therefore, the existence of excess capacity could prove to be an important factor in guarding against underservice by contract winners.

Little of the literature on competitive bidding explores the consequences for bidding behavior of selecting multiple winning bidders, where the bidders determine their own restrictions on the capacity of their bids. The Brimmer/Friedman articles discuss a situation— the Treasury Bill auction—with these characteristics, but do not systematically analyze their implications for bidding behavior and the revenue generated by the auctions. Also, Forsythe and Isaacs (1982) have proven theoretically that the submission of bids equal to actual costs is not necessarily a dominant bidding strategy in competitive auctions when bids can be constructed for multiple units.[21] However, some laboratory experiments indicate that bidders do still follow this approximate strategy in practice.[22] Smith's experimental results relating to Treasury Bill auctions suggest possible relationships between the number of rejected bids and auction revenues.[23] However, in Smith's experiment contracts were awarded to the highest bidders and participants were allowed to purchase at most two out of 18 available units. Therefore, the generalizability of Smith's results to competitive bidding for indigent medical care is unclear.

The Politics of Competitive Bidding System Design

The specification of design characteristics for indigent medical care bidding systems is a process that will inevitably be influenced by political, as well as technical, considerations. The likelihood that political considerations will play a major role in the process is enhanced by the ambiguity of the findings in the literature as they might apply to indigent medical care programs. Currently, as the discussion in this chapter suggests, program officials have limited theoretical and experimental research to employ in constructing bidding processes and defending these processes in the political arena. The remainder of this chapter identifies some important political considerations in the design of bidding system processes in general, and bidding for indigent medical care contracts in particular.

Obviously, any design for a competitive bidding system for indigent medical care will be politically controversial. There are entrenched provider and bureaucratic constituencies for existing indigent health care programs that will resist any changes that could redistribute patients or program resources. Every proposed bidding system design has a different distribution of benefits and costs associated with it and therefore will generate unique coalitions of supporters and opponents. However, in addition to this general political consideration, there are more limited issues related to specific alternative design elements and the manner in which they interact. For example, in its most familiar context competitive bidding is used to award one contract. The awarding of contracts to multiple providers in a given area, rather than a single winning bidder, raises a set of interesting political considerations relating to the choice of reimbursement alternatives for winning bidders.

From an economic point of view, the reimbursement of all winning bidders at the highest winning bid (the competitive auction rule) has several features to recommend it. It would encourage providers to submit bids reflecting their best cost estimates, thereby reducing incentives to "pad" bids, reduce costs associated with bid strategy formulation, and convey important information to the state concerning the actual costs of providing care to indigents. Furthermore, it would reward cost-effective innovations in medical care delivery, thus establishing incentives for system cost restraint in the long run. Despite these potential virtues, the adoption of competitive auction rules in any publicly financed competitive bidding system faces severe political problems.

First, reimbursement of providers in amounts exceeding their bids may conflict with existing state procurement laws. Second, reimbursement of all providers at the level of the highest winning bid gives the appearance of wastefulness on the part of the program's administrators and political supporters. Finally, and perhaps most importantly, the American public has ambivalent attitudes towards profits in general, and particularly towards profits generated through the delivery of medical care. While economists may view profit "as a necessary signal to draw capital and promote efficiency," the public is likely to see it as "making money from sick people" and "wasting the taxpayers' dollars."[24] This attitude is exacerbated by the relatively high income levels of physicians, the recipients of the profits.

While it might be possible to counteract the political liabilities of competitive auction rules if their potential advantages were certain, it would still be difficult to communicate these advantages effectively to the public in a way that would confer political benefits on supporters. For instance, the relative cost savings to the state from actual experience with competitive auction rules would be difficult to document, in the absence of comparable discriminative auction experience. Furthermore, some cost savings would occur gradually as competitors discovered and adopted new strategies for containing costs. Such cost savings are difficult to communicate to voters and may not be convincing in comparison with the apparently obvious "excess expenditures" involved in reimbursing all bidders at the level of the highest winning bid.

Even discriminative auction rules are not certain to emerge from the political process intact. On a procedural level, some state procurement laws may prohibit reimbursing providers at different amounts for the same service or accepting bids other than the lowest bid submitted. A more fundamental problem is that retention of a negotiation alternative has a strong political allure in the implementation of any bidding system, including a discriminative auction. When high bids are brought down to "acceptable" levels through "tough negotiation," program officials can point to "savings" that resulted from their "hard-nosed" management of the program. Unfortunately, any savings generated through negotiation after the submission of bids must be regarded as suspect, since a bidding process that allows subsequent negotiation encourages excessively high initial bids. Nevertheless, there will be political pressures for the state to negotiate or to adopt some other "bidding" alternative, such as an ascending Dutch auction, that gives the appearance of greater direct control over program expenditures.

Summary

For any competitive bidding process design to achieve its potential in containing costs, the state must be willing to accept the results of that design as valid. This means that program costs cannot be determined exactly in advance; they are generated as an outcome of the rules defining the bidding system. It is primarily this requirement that will make it politically difficult to maintain the effectiveness of any initial competitive bidding design for indigent medical care in the long run. It implies that the state must be committed to funding its indigent medical care program at the level of the winning bids. This places a great burden on program officials to design and administer appropriate "rules of the game" and to communicate the benefits of the rules effectively to potential bidders and to legislators. If they are not convinced that the incentives in the system are appropriate, program administrators will resist relinquishing the appearance of short-run "budgetary control" in return for the uncertain promise of future cost restraint. Currently, program officials have limited theoretical and experimental research that bears directly and unambiguously on bidding in indigent medical care programs to employ in structuring bidding processes and defending these processes in the political arena.

Notes

1. W. Vickrey, "Counterspeculation, Auctions and Competitive Sealed Tenders," *Journal of Finance* 16 (March 1961): 8–37.
2. For extensive bibliographies of the bidding literature see R. Engelbrecht-Wiggons, "Auctions and Bidding Models: A Survey," *Management Science* 26 (February 1980); or R. M. Starke, "Competitive Bidding: A Comprehensive Bibliography," *Operations Research* 19 (March-April 1971): 484–90.
3. Although this is considered the dominant strategy in a competitive auction under most conditions, there are situations where it is not optimal. See, for instance, R. Forsythe and R. M. Isaac, "Demand-Revealing Mechanisms for Private Goods Auctions," in V. L. Smith, ed., *Research in Experimental Economics, Vol. 2* (Greenwich, Connecticut: JAI Press, 1982).
4. A. F. Brimmer, "Price Determination in the United States Treasury Bill Market," *Review of Economics and Statistics* 44 (May 1962): 178–83; M. Friedman, "Price Determination in the United States Treasury Bill Market: A Comment," *Review of Economics and Statistics* 45 (August 1963): 318–20.
5. In most cases, the bidding literature pertains to situations where the highest bidder wins. In bidding for indigent medical care, or for construction or defense contracts, the lowest bid price determines the winning bidder. In our discussion, we present results as they were developed

by their authors and comment on their application to situations where the low bid wins as this seems necessary for the purposes of clarification.

6. J. G. Riley and W. F. Samuelson, "Optimal Auctions," *American Economic Review* 71 (June 1981): 381–92.

7. Ibid., p. 390.

8. J. B. Ramsey, *Bidding and Oil Leases* (Greenwich, Connecticut: JAI Press, 1980).

9. V. L. Smith, "Experimental Studies of Discrimination versus Competition in Sealed Bid Auction Markets," *Journal of Business* 40 (January 1967): 56–82.

10. G. J. Miller and C. R. Plott, "Revenue Generating Properties of Sealed Bid Auctions: An Experimental Analysis of One-Price and Discriminative Processes," in V. L. Smith, ed., *Research in Experimental Economics, Vol. 3* (Greenwich, Connecticut: JAI Press, 1983).

11. Vickrey, "Counterspeculation."

12. J. C. Cox, B. Roberson, and V. L. Smith, "Theory and Behavior of Single Object Auctions," in V. L. Smith, ed., *Research in Experimental Economics, Vol. 2* (Greenwich, Connecticut: JAI Press, 1982).

13. O. E. Williamson, "Franchise Bidding for National Monopolies—In General and with Respect to CATV," *Bell Journal of Economics* 7 (Spring 1976): 73–104.

14. Ibid., p. 84.

15. S. J. Rassenti, V. L. Smith, and R. L. Bulfin, "A Combinatorial Auction Mechanism for Airport Time Slot Allocation," *Bell Journal of Economics* 13 (Autumn 1982): 402–17.

16. K. M. Gaver and J. L. Zimmerman, "An Analysis of Competitive Bidding on BART Contracts," *Journal of Business* 50 (July 1977): 279–95.

17. A. K. Smiley, *Competitive Bidding Under Uncertainty: The Case of Offshore Oil* (Cambridge, Massachusetts: Ballinger, 1979).

18. Riley and Samuelson, "Optimal Auctions."

19. Smiley, *Competitive Bidding*.

20. K. C. Brown, *Bidding for Offshore Oil: Toward an Optimal Strategy* (Dallas: Southern Methodist University Press, 1969).

21. Forsythe and Isaac, "Demand-Revealing Mechanisms."

22. D. M. Grether, R. M. Isaac, and C. R. Plott, "Alternative Methods of Allocating Airport Slots: Performance and Evaluation," CAB Report Pasadena, CA: Polinomics Research Laboratories.

23. V. L. Smith, "Experimental Studies."

24. W. McClure, "Structure and Incentive Problems in Economic Regulation of Medical Care," *Milbank Memorial Fund Quarterly/Health and Society,* 59 (Spring 1981): 107–44.

5

Development of the Competitive Bidding System in Arizona

The implementation of public policy may result in programs vastly different from those envisioned by their legislative architects. In chapter 3, we described the legislative framework for AHCCCS, identifying those components of the competitive bidding system that were specified in the legislation, as well as those left to be formulated during implementation. In chapter 4, we summarized the findings of the extensive literature on the structure and incentives in various types of competitive bidding processes. In this chapter, we describe the events in the implementation of the AHCCCS competitive bidding system. A flow chart of implementation activities for the entire AHCCCS program guides the narrative to simplify a complex implementation process (figure 5.1). In the next chapter, we analyze the reasons for the various implementation decisions made by program administrators.

Activities Required to Implement AHCCCS

The basic activities required to implement the competitive bidding system for providers in AHCCCS began informally, immediately after the AHCCCS legislation became law. However, full-time staff and permanent quarters for the implementation team were not obtained until January 1982. Therefore, we begin our description of the implementation process on this date, and continue until the target operational date of October 1, 1982.

The activities necessary to implement AHCCCS can be subdivided into three separate sets of tasks, according to their relation to the provider procurement process. Those activities external to the development of the medical care delivery network produced few products needed for competitive bidding to proceed and may be viewed as essentially independent from the implementation of the bidding process. For example, the internal administration of the AHCCCS Division within the Arizona Department of Health Services (ADHS) was devoted mainly to start-up and oversight activities and included acquiring space, hiring staff and administrative leadership, developing functional relationships with other levels of the state bureaucracy, and developing appropriate audit programs, hearing and appeal provisions, fraud provisions, and other activities ultimately related to contract enforcement. The Coordination and Information Program provided public notice of proceedings through mailings and via the mass media and received feedback, via regional and statewide meetings, as AHCCCS developed. The Program Evaluation component of AHCCCS, which was not established until July 1983, had as its goal the documentation and evaluation of the effectiveness of the various cost-containment features of AHCCCS.

A second group of activities, while not geared specifically towards the competitive bidding process, is related to that process through shared products, tasks, approvals, or resources. These activities include promulgating rules and regulations to more fully define the conditions under which AHCCCS would be implemented, including a detailed methodology for competitive bidding; procuring the AHCCCS private administrator; preparing a written waiver request to be submitted to the Health Care Financing Administration (HCFA) of DHHS to gain exemption from certain Medicaid service requirements and thereby obtain federal funding for the program; and implementing eligibility determination and enrollment functions to ensure that adequate numbers of patients would be signed up with the winning bidders by October 1, 1982.

The competitive bidding process was itself composed of several components, each dependent on the other and, to some extent, on the activities described above. These components included preparing and issuing a request for proposal (RFP), or formal invitation to bid; preparing a model contract to provide potential bidders with some indication of the likely contractual requirements for participation in

Figure 5.1 Network of Activities Required to Implement AHCCS

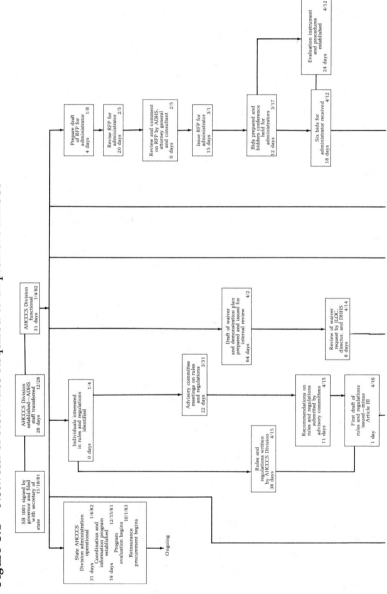

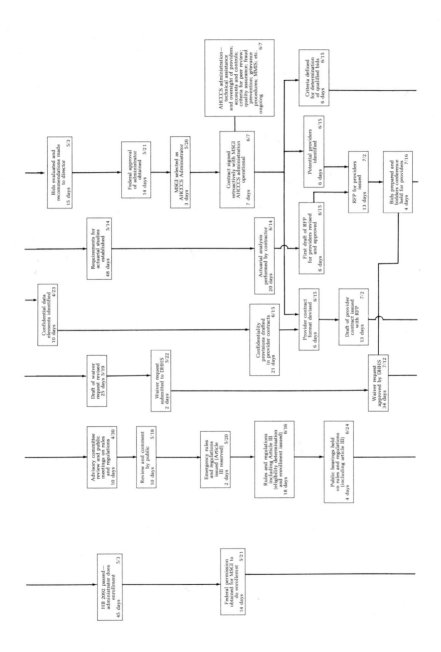

Bids evaluated and recommendations made to director
15 days   5/3

Federal approval of administrator obtained
14 days   5/21

MSGI selected as AHCCCS Administrator
3 days   5/26

Contract signed retroactively with MSGI AHCCCS administration operational
7 days   6/7

AHCCCS administration—technical assistance and oversight of providers; criteria for peer review; quality assurance; fraud prevention; grievance procedures; MMIS; etc. ongoing   6/7

Criteria defined for determination of qualified bids
6 days   6/15

Requirements for actuarial studies established
48 days   5/14

Actuarial analysis performed by contractor
20 days   6/14

Potential providers identified
6 days   6/15

First draft of RFP for providers reviewed and approved
6 days   6/15

RFP for providers issued
13 days   7/2

Bids prepared and bidders conference held for providers
4 days   7/16

Confidential data elements identified
10 days   4/23

Confidentiality provisions drafted in provider contracts
21 days   6/15

Provider contract format devised
6 days   6/15

Draft of provider contract issued with RFP
13 days   7/2

Draft of waiver request revised 5/19
25 days

Waiver request submitted to DHHS
2 days   5/22

Waiver request approved by DHHS
34 days   7/12

Advisory committee review and public meetings on rules and regulations
10 days   4/30

Review and comment by public
10 days   5/18

Emergency rules and regulations issued [Article III reserved]
2 days   5/20

Rules and regulations including Article III (eligibility determination and enrollment issued)
18 days   6/16

Public hearings held on rules and regulations (including article III)
4 days   6/24

HB 2002 passed—administrator does enrollment
45 days   5/3

Federal permission obtained for MSGI to do enrollment
14 days   5/21

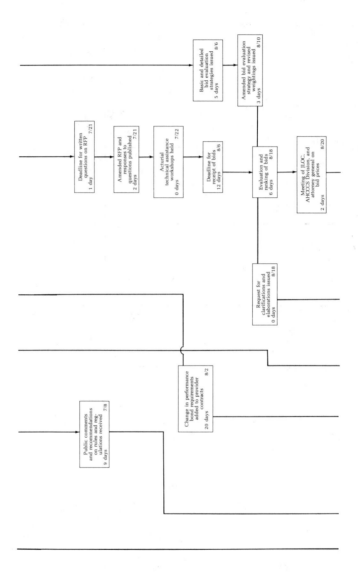

Figure 5.1 Continued

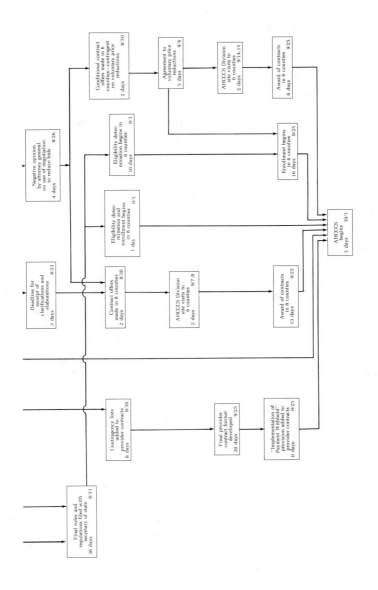

Final rules and
regulations filed with
secretary of state
38 days   8/31

Contingency lists
added to
provider contracts
8 days   8/30

Final provider
contract format
developed   9/25
20 days

"Implementation of
'Payment Withheld'
provision added to
provider contracts"
0 days   9/25

Deadline for
receipt of
clarifications and
elaborations   8/23
3 days

Contract offers
made in 8 counties
2 days   8/30

AHCCCS Division
site visits to
8 counties
2 days   9/7,8

Award of contracts
in 8 counties
13 days   9/25

Eligibility deter-
mination and
enrollment begins
in 8 counties
1 day   9/1

Eligibility deter-
mination begins in
6 counties
10 days   9/1

Enrollment begins
in 6 counties
16 days   9/25

Negative opinion
by attorney general
on use of negotiation
to reduce bids
4 days   8/26

Conditional contract
offers made in 6
counties—contingent
on voluntary price
reductions
2 days   8/30

Agreement to
voluntary price
reductions
5 days   9/4

AHCCCS Division
site visits to
6 counties
2 days   9/14,15

Award of contracts
in 6 counties
8 days   9/25

AHCCCS
begins
10/1
5 days

AHCCCS; developing a methodology and strategy for an objective evaluation of bids and application of that process to the first round of bids; and procuring reinsurance for providers through a third competitive bidding process.

A flowchart showing the time required, precedence, and interrelationships of the tasks necessary to implement the competitive bidding system is presented in figure 5.1. Individual boxes or "nodes" indicate an activity, as well as the date of its completion and number of days necessary for its completion. The activities external to the bidding process (AHCCCS Administration, Coordination and Information, Program Evaluation, and Procurement of Reinsurance) are depicted in the chart, but are not connected to bidding process activities.

Implementation of Activities Related to Competitive Bidding

Rules and Regulations

The preparation of AHCCCS rules and regulations, one activity related to the bidding process, was necessary to more fully develop the legislative intent behind AHCCCS and to set guidelines for the actual operation of the program. This process began, formally, on January 4, 1982, although efforts were made to identify staff, provider organizations, and individuals interested in providing input to the process prior to that time. Program areas addressed in the development of the rules and regulations included the scope of services to be offered by winning bidders; processes to be used for determination of eligibility and enrollment of members; the format and mechanisms for enforcement of contracts and subcontracts with providers; general provisions regarding the management of members and benefits; the role of the private administrator of AHCCCS; processes to be used for the management of grievances and appeals by members; and the rules governing the competitive bidding process. This last area included a discussion of the frequency of bidding, the qualifications of entities acceptable as bidders, the mechanisms for evaluation of bids, the amount and source of reinsurance to cover catastrophic medical care, and the nature of performance bond requirements or alternatives to insure the program in the event of financial default by a provider.

Ad hoc advisory committees, consisting of interested providers and consumers, were formed to address these program areas, and meetings were held throughout February and March 1982. The purpose of these meetings was to provide input to AHCCCS Division staff, who were simultaneously writing a working draft of the rules and regulations. Over 200 formal recommendations were made by the ad hoc advisory committees, with some of these recommendations incorporated into the draft issued on April 15, 1982. Ad hoc advisory committee members were invited to comment on the draft rules and regulations by April 30 so that preparation of a second draft could commence. Review and comment by the ad hoc advisory committees, legislators, JLOC, professional associations, county and state officials, attorney general, and the public indicated that most sections of the rules and regulations were either acceptable as they stood in the draft, so similar to the legislation that change was not possible, or so controversial that consensus was impossible to achieve within the tight implementation schedule. Those remaining sections that were amenable to immediate change were revised by AHCCCS Division staff, but on May 20 it was necessary to issue emergency rules and regulations, which legally could remain in effect for 90 days, so that implementation of the program could move forward. In particular, the portion of the program rules and regulations dealing with eligibility determination and enrollment (Article III) proved to be so complex and controversial that staff found it necessary to reserve that section for release in a later draft.

The next draft of rules and regulations, which included a discussion of eligibility determination and enrollment, was released on June 16, 1982. The sections regulating the program administrator and the bidding process were not developed in any further detail, since there was considerable concern about their potential to discourage bidders, particularly in rural counties. Most of the individuals involved in preparing the rules and regulations believed that the competitive bidding process would benefit from the added flexibility provided by definition of bidding rules at a later date, as part of the request for proposals that would be sent to prospective bidders. Therefore, specific information regarding the format of bids, the evaluation process, frequency of bidding, and contractual requirements of providers was not included in the rules and regulations in effect at the time of bidding. Public hearings on the additions to the emergency rules and regulations were held, comments and recommendations were received, and final rules and regulations were filed with the secretary of state on August 31, 1982.

Waiver Request

Informal preparation of the AHCCCS plan for the demonstration project and waivers began before the AHCCCS legislation was passed. State lawmakers and legislative staff spent the spring and summer of 1981 discussing with federal officials the types of exemptions from federal Medicaid requirements that were likely to be acceptable to HCFA, DHHS, and the White House. This information was incorporated into the ultimate waiver request. Once implementation began, interactions between HCFA and AHCCCS staff provided information to allow revisions and expansion that would make the waiver request an approvable document. Therefore, the working draft issued for internal review on April 2 had the benefit of at least some input from those individuals who would be responsible, ultimately, for its approval. On November 19, 1981, Burton Barr, Arizona House Majority Leader, received a letter from the deputy administrator of HCFA stating that "if the State submits a technically acceptable [waiver request] to HCFA following these guidelines, we should be able to proceed to implement the demonstration." Thus, preparation of the waiver request proceeded with the expectation that formal approval was simply a technical hurdle.

Review of various drafts of the waiver request by the JLOC, the attorney general and AHCCCS Division staff and director occurred during April and May 1982, and the final document was submitted to HCFA on May 22, with the understanding that the Waiver Request will be formally acted upon within 30 days (21 working days) of the date of submittal. AHCCCS officials believed throughout the spring of 1982 that the maximum amount of "slippage" or delay that was acceptable, if AHCCCS were to be implemented on time, was five days. Because the timing of the waiver request was so critical to the effort to implement AHCCCS on schedule, the state AHCCCS Division director maintained daily contact with federal officials to be sure that there were no problems hindering timely approval. On June 10, it became apparent through these unofficial communications that there was going to be a delay, due to the need for final approval by the Office of Management and Budget (OMB).

While OMB's approval of all such waiver requests is normally a formality, the fact that Arizona was not a participant in Medicaid at that time raised a question of whether the federal government would have to supply an additional $19 million in AFDC enhancement and income maintenance funds, which were not included in the existing federal budget but would normally accompany Medicaid programs. Arizona officials assumed that receipt of Title XIX funds would automatically bring in these additional dollars, but OMB questioned this position and delayed action on the waiver request beyond the expected date of approval. Efforts by the AHCCCS Division director, legislative sponsors of AHCCCS, White House representatives, and officials at HCFA to gain approval were ultimately successful, but not until July 12, three weeks after the scheduled date. Considerable work and time were expended in this effort by the state AHCCCS Division, resulting in fewer resources available for other implementation activities.

Approval of the waiver request by the federal government was necessary for three other processes to occur (shown on figure 5.1), each of which was interdependent and crucial to the timely implementation of AHCCCS: receipt of $50 million in federal funds to pay for services beginning on October 1, 1982; formal federal approval of the choice of McAuto Systems Group, Incorporated (MSGI) as AHCCCS private administrator, which required prior approval of the waiver request; and implementation of the bidding process, which included preparation of bids by providers. The latter was seen by AHCCCS officials to be contingent upon federal approval of the waiver request, since it appeared unlikely that potential providers would attempt the costly and time-consuming process of bidding without the formal assurance that federal funds would, in fact, be available to finance the program. While the actual availability of funds was not affected by the waiver delay, the delay did necessitate retroactive approval of the administrator's contract and written personal guarantees by the Division director that the administrator's operating costs would be reimbursed for the period June 7 through July 12, regardless of the federal government's decision.

The delay also resulted in a one-week postponement of the release of the invitation for providers to bid, allowing providers five rather than six weeks for the preparation of bids and the design of a bid evaluation strategy. In addition, MSGI was reluctant to expend significant resources without a signed contract, so they provided only skeleton staff and consultants to the bidding process during the first year. The intent of the AHCCCS legislation was that the administrator be fully responsible for implementation of the bidding process. As a consequence of the delay in approval of the waiver request, and the corresponding late execution of the administrator's contract, significant involvement of AHCCCS Division staff in the bidding process was needed, and the transition of power and authority from state staff to the administrator had to occur while the bidding process was also taking place.

The Procurement Process
for the AHCCCS Administrator

Selection of the AHCCCS administrator was a high priority process because of the central role defined by the legislation for that organization in all of AHCCCS, and particularly the competitive bidding process (figure 5.1). Therefore, a concerted effort was made to complete the selection process quickly so that a contract could be signed by May 1982, prior to bid formulation by providers. As shown in figure 5.1, a preliminary draft of the request for proposal (RFP) for administrator was ready for revision and review by ADHS administrative staff, the attorney general, and a consultant hired for that purpose on February 5. Revisions were completed and the RFP was issued on March 1. AHCCCS Division staff developed procedures, criteria, and an evaluation instrument to be used in selection of the administrator during the time when bids were being prepared. Six bids were received on April 12, and the following three weeks were used for evaluation of bids. Preliminary recommendations were then made to the AHCCCS Division director (who had been selected immediately before the bidding process for the administrator began). The bidders made oral presentations of their proposals before an AHCCCS Division evaluation team on May 12, with the division director subsequently selecting McAuto Systems Group as the program administrator. While official federal approval of the contract award had to wait for approval of the waiver request (on July 12), verbal approval of the choice by federal officials was obtained on May 21. Formal notification to winning and losing bidders and the public was made on May 26, and the contract was actually awarded on May 29.

Since contract negotiations and federal approval of the award and waiver request were still in progress, MSGI started work on the competitive bidding process and other implementation activities with only minimal staff, in temporary quarters, between May 26 and June 7. The administrator was authorized to begin work on June 7 by the

AHCCCS Division director but, in the absence of a written contract, MSGI was reticent about increasing the resources it committed to the program. When final approval of the contract was received (July 30), MSGI began to devote significant personnel and resources to the administration of AHCCCS.

Eligibility Determination and Enrollment

The development of eligibility determination and enrollment procedures was related to competitive bidding because potential bidders viewed them as important in their efforts to construct estimates of enrollment and total capitation payments. Furthermore, uncertainty surrounding these procedures reflected negatively on the competence of AHCCCS officials to implement the program on time and to supply adequate enrollees to ensure the financial viability of winning bidders. An open enrollment period of 30 days was seen as essential to process the projected number of potential eligibles, necessitating the start of eligibility determination and enrollment on September 1. The fact that the eligibility and enrollment section of the rules and regulations was not available until June 16 was of some concern to bidders. Furthermore, legislators decided to add the task of patient enrollment to the private administrator's other responsibilities under the assumption that the private administrator was better able to play the role of unbiased information broker. Thus, H.B. 2092 was passed on May 3, and federal approval of this change in the functions of MSGI was received on May 21. Eligibility determination began as scheduled, but problems with bid prices (as discussed below) allowed enrollment to proceed in only eight of the 14 counties on that date. Enrollment was not started in the remaining six counties until September 25, less than one week before AHCCCS was to begin delivering services. As a result, low total first month capitation payments to providers were the rule in most counties, reflecting low enrollments in plans.

Implementation of the
Competitive Bidding Process

Overview of Competitive Bidding Process

Implementation of the competitive bidding process for AHCCCS providers did not actually begin until June 7, when MSGI became involved, albeit marginally, in the administration of AHCCCS (figure 5.1). Until that time, the AHCCCS Division director and staff attempted, informally, to conceptualize how the competitive bidding process might take place. Experts were invited to share their expertise, seminars were held, but no firm decisions were made on what bidding or evaluation techniques would be used. Implementors believed that an actuarial analysis of the available population, utilization, and cost figures for indigent care in each county was necessary. Therefore, requirements for those studies were established from March 10 until May 14, and an analysis was completed by a consultant under contract on June 14. This analysis was provided to potential bidders in the request for proposals (RFP), issued on July 2. Several implementors thought that any thorough consideration of bidding techniques was fruitless prior to the time bids were received (on August 6), since their major concern focused on inducing providers to bid. Concurrence with this belief was reflected in the emergency rules and regulations, which contained only a paraphrasing of the legislative wording on the competitive bidding process and no further conceptualization of bidding or evaluation methodology. The competitive bidding process began with the release of the request for provider services (RFP) on July 2, 1982. Preliminary drafts of this document were approved by a review committee, the AHCCCS Division director, the attorney general, and the legislature.

Invitation to Bid

The release of the RFP for provider services on July 2 was preceded by identification and notification of potential bidding organizations (June 7 through June 15). The RFP contained information about the bidding process that was not available previously to potential bidders, including the amount of time contracts would be in effect, lists of service requirements, and actuarial data related to potential service use. Also, bid sheets were provided for the calculation of bid prices for each population. Providers began preparation of bids, and those with questions on the bidding process or structure of bids attended a bidders conference on July 21. Actuarial technical assistance workshops were held in three locations in Arizona on July 20, 21, and 22 to help bidders utilize the actuarial data contained in the proposal in the construction of their bid prices.

While providers were constructing their bids, AHCCCS officials made several decisions that modified or clarified various aspects of the legislation. For instance, they stated their intention to make more than one award in each county, provided that there were multiple qualified bidders and bid prices were "reasonable." While this intent had been expressed by legislators, it was not clearly stated in the legislation itself. AHCCCS officials diverged significantly from the stipulations of the legislation when they defined new population groups for which bids would be submitted. Providers were told that contract awards would be based on these new groupings (AFDC, disabled, blind, aged, and medically needy/medically indigent), rather than the legislatively mandated groups. Thus, while bids were submitted for employed groups under AHCCCS they were not evaluated in the initial bidding process. Finally, AHCCCS officials stated a preference for full service bids; that is, those bids that encompassed under one price all categories of service defined by the law. This decision was designed to minimize the time and resources the private administrator would need to devote to "network formation". The deadline for receipt of bids was August 6. On this date, 113 bids, including 39 full service bids, were submitted to AHCCCS officials. To the surprise of many, all 14 counties in Arizona received at least one full service bid.

Bid Evaluation and Contract Award Process

On August 5, the day before provider bids were due, MSGI issued a basic bid evaluation strategy for review by the AHCCCS Division. State staff regarded this form as too simplistic and subjective and requested a more detailed, objective evaluation instrument. This second document was produced by MSGI on August 6 (two hours before the deadline for receipt of bids) and was composed of a three-part numerical questionnaire to be completed by three independent bid evaluation teams. This more objective bid evaluation strategy was amended and supplemented on August 10 by a document giving instructions for development of a composite bid by the weighting of appropriate combinations of eligible populations. This composite bid was then used by teams of evaluators from the AHCCCS Division, MSGI, and consulting firms to help rank bidders by price, the dominant criterion, in addition to "qualification" and "technical acceptability."

On August 18, a letter was sent to all providers requesting "clarifications and elaborations" of portions of their bids (excluding price). The deadline for receipt of these documents was August 23.

While bidders were responding to this request, program officials determined that the AHCCCS budget was insufficient to cover projected costs, based on bid prices in six of Arizona's 14 counties. AHCCCS and MSGI staff met with the JLOC and the attorney general to determine how to resolve this problem. The AHCCCS director suggested that negotiation with providers over price be used to help reduce program costs, but the legality of such a technique was questioned. It was determined by the attorney general, who had not been involved in AHCCCS implementation to any substantial degree prior to this time, that state procurement precedents did not allow for direct negotiation with bidders over price. Instead, he suggested that a request for "voluntary price reductions" by bidders in these six counties would be acceptable and would probably not result in legal challenges. If voluntary price reductions were not sufficient to meet the AHCCCS budget, the director would have to reject all bids in each of the six counties and conduct another round of bidding. However, the alternative of rebidding would have delayed the start of AHCCCS and damaged the program's financial viability and public credibility. Therefore, on August 30, contract offers were made in eight counties and conditional contract offers, contingent on voluntary price reductions, were made in the remaining counties, with a due date of September 4.

Once contract offers had been made in eight counties, eligibility determination and enrollment began in those counties on September 1, as scheduled. However, since providers had not yet submitted voluntary price reductions in the remaining six counties, only eligibility determination could begin there. After contract offers had been made in eight counties, AHCCCS Division teams visited provider sites to substantiate and validate proposals (September 7 and 8). Voluntary price reductions were received by the AHCCCS Division on September 4 from bidders in the remaining six counties and were judged sufficient to allow the program to operate within its projected budget. Site visits took place (September 14 and 15), and on September 25 enrollment began in these counties and awards of contracts to all providers were announced. As a result of the competitive bidding process, contracts ultimately were awarded in all 14 counties, with multiple winning bidders in nine counties containing 91 percent of the state's population.

Delivery of services financed by AHCCCS began on October 1, but a significant number of details remained to be resolved before contracts could be signed. Subcontracting arrangements with hospitals, pharmacies, labs, specialists, and other providers by primary care provider groups, who represented the majority of bidders, remained to be arranged. In addition, the details of many contracts were not settled until well into October. Both providers and AHCCCS officials operated on faith that the winning bidders would deliver appropriate services although not yet under formal contract.

Contract Design

Included with the RFP, issued on July 2, was a model contract that would be used to legally define contractual requirements of all parties involved. The model contract was based on revisions of previous drafts (prepared prior to June 15). After the RFP had been released, implementors realized that it would be difficult for newly formed consortia of providers to obtain performance bonds from traditional insurers to guarantee performance of the terms of their contracts. Therefore, on August 2, potential bidders were informed that, as an alternative to a traditional performance bond, the state would, on request, delay payments to the contractors for 30 days, representing 1/12 of their annual capitation payments. This amount would provide funds for the state to obtain sufficient fee-for-service coverage for almost one month in the event of contractor failure. Additional modification of the provider contracts took place after bids had been evaluated and winning bidders identified. On August 30, contingency lists specifying provisions required of individual providers were added to each contract, based on the perceived inadequacies of the proposals of bidding organizations. The final contract format was developed on September 25, and a one-page "implementation of payment withheld" provision was added to each. This document clarified the performance bond alternative contained in the contract and indicated whether the provider elected that option over a traditional performance bond. While AHCCCS began on October 1, contracts were signed, retroactively, during subsequent weeks, and providers delivered services initially without signed contracts.

Summary

The ten-month time frame established for implementation of the AHCCCS provided a major challenge to program officials. The implementation activities that required the cooperation of actors over whom implementors had the least control, and thus were most susceptible to unanticipated delays, were federal approval of the waiver request, submission of bids by providers, and assumption of administrative responsibility by a private administrator. Federal approval of the waiver request was delayed by three weeks, resulting in a delay in activation of the private administrator's contract and a delay in initiation of the provider procurement process. Unexpectedly high bid prices submitted by some providers called for the involvement of the attorney general in AHCCCS, a request for voluntary price reductions in six counties, and a subsequent delay in enrollment in these counties. The delay in assumption of responsibility by MSGI resulted in the transfer of responsibility from AHCCCS Division to MSGI at a critical time when implementation resources were particularly scarce. The reasons for the key implementation decisions identified in this chapter, as well as the likely effects of these decisions for program performance, are discussed in chapter 6.

6

An Analysis of the Arizona Experience in Implementing a Competitive Bidding Process

The process of translating a law into an actual program—the implementation process—can be influenced by many factors. This chapter analyzes the implementation of the competitive bidding component of the Arizona experiment, with two objectives in mind. First, it is intended to be useful in identifying those factors that are likely to be important in the implementation of competitive bidding systems in other states or for different purposes. A second, more general objective is to enhance the understanding of policy analysts and public sector decision makers of how the implementation process can affect the ability of competitive reforms in public sector programs to achieve their potential for cost containment.

Although there is only a limited literature addressing the actual implementation of competition in public medical care programs, numerous published studies have analyzed the implementation experience of other public sector programs. There is also a separate, but very extensive, literature, described in chapter 4, on the structure and incentives in various types of competitive bidding processes.[1] We draw

This chapter was previously published as part of an article in the *Journal of Health Politics, Policy and Law*, Fall 1984.

upon results from both areas to identify factors that, in our judgment, had a significant impact on the development of the competitive bidding process as described in chapter 5. Then we analyze the experience in Arizona with respect to each of these factors, deriving conclusions concerning their relative importance. In conclusion, we discuss why the standard model of competitive bidding was not implemented in Arizona. We suggest that straightforward competitive bidding systems will be difficult to implement as cost-containment mechanisms in indigent medical care programs because of several fundamental implementation problems uncovered in the Arizona experiment.

Methodology

Shortell and Solomon state, "It is interesting that, while there have been a number of significant contributions detailing the development of health care policies, relatively little attention has been given to the implementation of health care policy."[2] The implementation analyses that do exist utilize a variety of theoretical frameworks depending on study objectives. None of these past approaches is ideally suited for analysis of the implementation of the Arizona bidding process. However, they do contain a number of common themes, or broadly defined factors, that can be of some value in predicting potential problem implementation areas.[3] Based on a review of frequently cited studies, factors identified by others as pertinent to program implementation were grouped into categories for the analysis in this chapter.

Categorization of Explanatory Factors

Van Meter and Van Horn, Mead, Hargrove, Edwards, and Rourke each provide portions of a framework for studying the implementation of the AHCCCS bidding system.[4] Van Meter and Van Horn develop a conceptual model of the policy implementation process containing specific "variables that shape the linkage between policy and performance."[5] Mead describes a series of variables or "explanatory factors for implementation problems," which are important to the analysis of implementation problems within Medicaid.[6] Hargrove adopts a more abstract approach to analysis of the implementation process and describes the kinds of knowledge needed to understand how the implementation process affects the ultimate delivery of services in social programs. He notes the importance for policy implementation of "environmental factors," such as resources, technology, and characteristics of the individuals to be served.[7] In his study of implementation, Edwards identifies four factors he considers preconditions and possible obstacles to successful implementation: communication, resources, dispositions or attitudes, and bureaucratic structure.[8] He notes that there is interaction between and among these factors, which may complicate implementaion. Finally, Rourke studies the implementing agencies themselves to provide insights into the implementation process. While Rourke does not focus on many of the factors seen as important by others, he does provide insights into the importance of agency power, expertise, and esprit, as well as "environmental" factors such as the media and judicial rulings, for program implementation.[9]

These authors identify a wide variety of factors as critical to an analysis of program implementation, and their studies, taken together, define a framework for classifying factors important to the implementation of the competitive bidding process in Arizona. The four categories of factors addressed in the following analysis are: features of the environment; availability of resources; political forces; and characteristics of bureaucracies, including organizational features, dispositions of implementors, and communications among agencies (table 6.1).

Data

According to Yin, "exemplary studies of implementation" with which one might "gain some confidence about the validity and generalizability of the lessons to be learned" all collect evidence from multiple sources, analyze the data using multiple methodologies, and have both internal and external credibility.[10] In this chapter we have relied on the literature on policy implementation discussed above to provide a framework for our analysis. Data were collected in a series of structured and open-ended interviews of legislators and staff, governor's staff, assistant attorneys general, consultants to AHCCCS, providers who were bidders and potential bidders, and lobbyists for and against AHCCCS.[11] Quantitative data on the status of bidders, the utilization and cost assumptions in bids, and the demographic characteristics of Arizona counties were also analyzed. Finally, press releases and documents published by state government pertaining to the competitive bidding system, as well as articles published in Arizona newspapers and journals, were reviewed. Thus, the analysis reflects

Table 6.1 Explanatory Factors Influencing Implementation

Authors	Environment	Resources	Politics	Characteristics of Bureaucracies			Other
				Organizational Features	Dispositions of Implementors	Communication between Agencies	
Mead	Background economic and social forces	Funding levels only	Federalism; conflict with other programs; interest groups; due process	Administrative weaknesses			Incentive structure; weaknesses of provider institutions
Van Meter and Van Horn	Economic and social environment	Policy resources; interorganizational enforcement activities	Political environment	Character of implementing agencies	Dispositions of implementors; goal consensus; amount of change	Interorganizational communication activities	Policy standards and objectives
Hargrove	Technology; characteristics of clients	Resources (considered by Hargrove an environmental factor)	Political acceptability of policy; politics of implementation	Functioning of organizations			Design of policy; performance of professionals; dynamic relationship between citizens and government
Edwards		Staff; facilities; authority; information		Structure of agency	Dispositions or attitudes	Transmission; clarity; consistency	
Rourke	Media and judicial influences	Agency expertise		Agency power	Organizational esprit; leadership		

a wide variety of views and sources of information concerning how competitive bidding in AHCCCS was implemented.

Analysis of the Implementation Process

The analysis is organized by the categories of factors identified in the literature review and summarized in table 6.1. For each category, the potential importance of each specific factor is discussed and contrasted with our perception of its actual importance to implementation of the competitive bidding process in Arizona.

Environmental Forces

Environmental forces are factors that are external to the implementation process but may affect that process indirectly through their ability to influence the public sector in general and the agencies responsible for implementation in particular. For instance, recessionary economic conditions may result in greater numbers of unemployed, eligible clients for a particular program, causing budgetary problems for program implementation. Or, unanticipated inflation may alter total projected program costs in a variety of ways that affect implementation.[12] Society's attitudes towards a particular public program also constitute a potentially important environmental factor. For example, the nature of the clients to be served by a program, such as the elderly, the poor, or the mentally ill, can elicit different degrees of support for implementation activities.[13] Finally, the attitudes of the media can have an uncertain, and largely uncontrollable, effect on program implementation. The press can portray an innovative program as "exciting" or as "a dangerous gamble." The latter position can put program implementors on the defensive and make them prone to excessively cautious action. Also "while agencies and the media . . . have a common stake in the dissemination of news, they differ radically in their perceptions of what should be disclosed."[14] Thus, ill-timed or premature releases of sensitive details of policies may bring about ill-timed or premature decisions by implementors.

  The economic environment in Arizona during the passage of the AHCCCS legislation was relatively favorable, with generally lower unemployment rates than prevailed in the rest of the nation. This suggested that the number of potential program eligibles would be fairly stable over the demonstration period. However, two specific events occurred during implementation that created a great deal of uncertainty concerning the total number of individuals who would actually qualify for enrollment with winning provider groups. Copper mines laid off the majority of miners in the state during June 1982, resulting in a statewide increase in the number of potential AHCCCS eligibles. Worldwide inflation caused devaluation of the Mexican peso, resulting in a probable, but unpredictable, increased migration of Mexican nationals to Arizona. At the same time, unemployment levels began to rise due to decreased construction and retail sales caused by the recessionary climate nationally. The resulting increase in the number of potential eligibles meant unpredictably higher program costs for the state, increasing political pressures for the initial round of bidding to generate "low bids." It also created uncertainty about the distribution of enrollees across the various categories for which providers were required to submit bids. While this uncertainty may have affected the decisions of some providers to participate in the bidding process or the levels of submitted bids, it was not identified as a major concern by most bidders.

Prevailing social attitudes towards indigent programs in particular, and public programs in general, also played a role in a number of implementation decisions. Arizona voters traditionally have supported local autonomy and opposed an increased federal presence in the state. This was reflected in the history of opposition to the traditional Medicaid model as described in chapter 2. AHCCCS was promoted by legislators as a state alternative to federal programs and as a way to save costs and introduce private market constraints into the delivery of medical care. As such, it was consistent with societal attitudes.

However, these same attitudes constrained the manner in which program managers could deal with potential cost overruns. In prior elections, Arizona voters tended to support candidates opposed to generous welfare benefits, resulting in stringent income requirements for participation in indigent programs. They also supported legislation that restricted the revenue-generating abilities of state and local governments. Therefore, state politicians were wary of any implementation activities that could expand benefit packages or relax eligibility criteria. They also were extremely concerned that the sum of the contract awards that resulted from the bidding process stay within budgeted levels for the program. Thus, from the early stages of implementation, the concept of "negotiation" after bids were submitted, while it was not addressed explicitly in the program legislation or rules and regulations, had a strong attractiveness for politicians and implementors as a means of avoiding potential cost overruns. (The generic nature of this attractiveness was discussed in chapter 4).

Judicial rulings may also have affected program implementation in the Arizona experiment. A U.S. Supreme Court ruling, which declared that illegal immigrants were eligible for publicly funded education in Texas (June 1982), called into question the plans of policymakers and implementors to exclude these individuals from participation in AHCCCS. Thus, the number of potential eligibles again grew beyond levels used initially in estimating total program costs. This judicial ruling, when combined with increased unemployment and devaluation of the peso, created skepticism in the minds of potential bidders concerning the fiscal integrity of the program. Bidder skepticism, as well as a lack of reliable data on costs and utilization for program eligibles, caused implementors to be concerned that the number of bidders would be insufficient to establish competition. The preference expressed by program implementors for multiple winning bidders in each county was motivated in part by this concern. However, while it may have induced more providers to bid in the initial round, it may also have decreased the cost-containment potential of the bidding process. In rural counties, providers could submit relatively high bids and still be assured of participating in the program, since the number of potential bidders was small.

In Arizona, the media were both supportive and critical of AHCCCS during its implementation. While some newspapers stressed the potential for Arizona to lead the nation in health care reform, others emphasized the problems that surfaced during the implementation stage with headlines such as "Health-care plan is Kino [Pima County Hospital] nightmare,"[15] "Unready health-care plan may debut October 1,"[16] and "New health-plan picture cloudy for rural poor."[17] Such press coverage may have influenced the decisions of some providers concerning participation in the bidding process, although there is no indication that this occurred. However, it certainly drained valuable AHCCCS staff time in efforts to repair credibility damaged by negative news reports.

In summary, the competitive bidding system in AHCCCS was affected by environmental factors primarily through the imposition of even greater uncertainty than was anticipated at the program's inception. Local economic events and a coincidental Supreme Court decision diminished bidder confidence in estimates of costs, utilization, and numbers of potential enrollees in the program. The necessity for implementors to react to unfavorable media coverage meant a reallocation of scarce staff time away from program development. More importantly for program implementation, these environmental factors increased the likelihood that outcomes of the bidding process would be viewed as "unacceptable" by policymakers and implementors, since they created pressures to demonstrate cost containment at an early stage in the program's development.

Resources

Hargrove, Mead, and Pressman and Wildavsky consider "resources" to be external to the institutions responsible for implementation;[18] they are simply those limited funds specified by law to purchase or deliver services to clients of social programs. In this context, the implementation process is affected only by the extent to which the available funds are limited in comparison with actual or projected program costs. In analysis of the implementation of the competitive bidding process, resources are defined more broadly to include such things as space for program management and service delivery, equipment and supplies, availability of staff in adequate numbers and with appropriate levels of expertise, information or the means to obtain adequate information, the authority of implementors to enforce contract compliance by providers, and the time available to complete required implementation tasks.

Edwards considered inadequacies in staffing a principal source of implementation failure.[19] Low salaries, dictated by inadequate funding, may result in high turnover rates or the hiring of staff with inadequate training or skills. Also, hiring of too few staff, regardless of expertise or interest in the program, may result in a high turnover rate due to "burnout." The available funds for initial policy implementation by the AHCCCS Division (within Arizona state government) were set at $500,000 by the legislature, but the group winning the competitively bid program management contract was to be paid at the level of its bid. Once this contract was signed, costs of administering AHCCCS were theoretically fixed in both implementing agencies.[20] However, delays in finalizing the MSGI contract affected the availability of staff to implement the bidding process. One of the first activities faced by MSGI staff was to help design and implement the competitive bidding system in June/July 1982. But only skeleton staff and few consultants were employed by MSGI during this period since formal approval for Arizona's waiver request had not yet been obtained. MSGI staff members involved in the competitive bidding process were new to the AHCCCS in general and to the bidding process in particular. As a result, state AHCCCS Division staff became actively involved in this process, resulting in some diffusion of focus and confusion of responsibility between the two separate groups of implementors.[21]

Information, or the means to obtain information, can be considered an important resource that is sometimes related to adequate funding and staffing. In Arizona, the lack of information available to providers concerning the competitive bidding process affected program implementation. Prior to the submission of bids, data on numbers of potential eligibles in each enrollment group, the costs of providing service, and the potential utilization of enrollees in each of Arizona's counties were generally regarded as unreliable. Consequently, potential bidders had little confidence in the estimates supplied by the state. This lack of reliable information probably increased bid prices and reduced the number of providers who submitted bids.

The authority of the implementing agency to take those actions necessary for program implementation can also be considered a resource, and the lack of authority to enforce necessary implementation activities proved a problem for AHCCCS implementation.[22] The ultimate responsibility for implementing the bidding system resided, in theory, with the AHCCCS Division director within state government. However, the authority to design and implement the competitive bidding process was restricted by the attorney general and by the members and staff of the Joint Legislative Oversight Committee, which was created to monitor the program's development. There was also considerable ambiguity in the division of authority between the director of the state AHCCCS Division and MSGI. As described in chapter 3, the administrator had substantial legislated contractual authority in the following areas: developing a management information system to inform program evaluation and future bidding activities; providing technical assistance for potential bidders when requested; constructing an adequate, objective methodology for the evaluation of bids; and preparing a model contract acceptable to the AHCCCS Division and the Department of Administration. While state staff often viewed MSGI activities in these areas as deficient, their ability to impose sanctions on the administrator was restricted by the support for MSGI expressed by important figures in state government. In practice, the Division director's authority over the program administrator was quite limited. Within the context of the competitive bidding process, the effect was to create confusion among providers concerning program leadership. This confusion was compounded by negative newspaper articles relating to MSGI's performance.[23]

Time itself must be considered a scarce resource for implementation. The time period designated for start-up and planning should be sufficient to allow for the uncertainty, delays, and "slippage" that are inherent in the implementation of new programs. Frequently, the concepts used in the design of innovative programs are complex and require adequate time for comprehension by implementors. Simply adding more staff in such cases will not help but, instead, may confuse issues and result in compromise that may weaken program design.

The consensus of program implementors was that ten months constituted an insufficient period in which to establish a statewide service delivery system through competitive bidding. As described in the previous chapter, several unanticipated problems that arose during implementation contributed to the inadequacy of the original implementation time frame: late approval by HCFA of the waiver request, under which federal funds were made available for program operations; problems in contract negotiations with MSGI; a shift in the locus of responsibility for enrollment of clients from the state AHCCCS Division to MSGI; delayed transfer of responsibility for program administration from the AHCCCS Division to the administrator; and unexpectedly high bid levels that resulted in additional, unanticipated implementation measures to stay within the program's target budget.

The initial, compressed time frame and the unanticipated delays noted above affected the implementation process in a variety of ways. For instance, the shortage of time between the hiring of the first staff by MSGI (June 7, 1982) and delivery of services (October 1, 1982) precluded thorough examination by all staff of the complex issues involved in the design of bidding processes; the extreme demands imposed by the necessity to establish a provider network in a short time period crowded out other considerations.[24] Also, MSGI was unable to provide an objective, quantitative instrument for evaluation of the quality, technical acceptability, and relative price of bids until the day provider bids were received. Again, pressure of time and other limited resources, as well as delayed transfer of responsibility, were to blame. The lack of a published evaluation instrument created uncertainty among providers and may have inflated bids. Several providers suggested that they "padded" their bids to compensate for this uncertainty and to allow for possible future negotiation over price. Finally, time pressures also contributed to a decision on the part of program administrators to separate the bidding process for indigents from the submission of bids for county and state employees and private groups. The indigent bidding process received first priority since federal funding was tied to its successful completion. Bidding for nonindigents was postponed and, in fact, never successfully accomplished.

While complaints were often voiced concerning time constraints and the pressures they placed on implementors, in some ways the implementation process may have been simplified by these time limitations. Since there was little time available for the "luxury" of debate concerning many of the controversial features of the program, it was difficult for interest groups to mobilize support or opposition to key decisions rapidly enough to affect the implementation process. The lack of available time restricted the number of decision makers who could become involved in many key program decisions and also may have reduced the number of actual "decision points."[25] Therefore, the implementation process was, in a sense, streamlined by the presence of a deadline and the speed at which implementation necessarily proceeded.

It is reasonable to conclude that implementation of the competitive bidding process in AHCCCS clearly was restricted by insufficient resources. Limited staff resources at the time the bidding system was devised, coupled with a largely unavoidable lack of appropriate information and expertise, resulted in uncertainty among implementors and potential bidders concerning the design and operation of the bidding process. The lack of AHCCCS Division authority that was, in practice, commensurate with its responsibilities resulted in less assistance for potential bidders than was intended. Finally, time constraints served to hinder implementation in some ways, but expedited it in others. Rapid implementation resulted in limited consideration of alternative bidding rules and evaluation procedures but may have restricted the ability of interest groups to block or retard the bidding process.

Political Forces

The politics of the implementation process must be distinguished from the politics of the policy-making process, because the actors, goals, and nature of the two processes are different. As explained by

Hargrove, policymaking is "aggregative in character through the creation of coalitions for agreement," while "in the implementation process the consensus required for decision comes unstuck and support for the program fragments among separated groups of actors who engage in isolated maneuvers and counter-maneuvers."[26] That is, unified actions taken by legislators, the executive branch, the bureaucracy, and interest groups to pass legislation may be reversed during implementation, when each group fights for control over portions of the program.[27]

Elected Officials. Hargrove suggests that the influence of policymakers on implementation is normally limited and their incentives to exercise influence are weak. As an elected official, the policymaker must be responsive to the pressures of constituents, whose interests are more likely to be aroused by the intent of a policy rather than its implementation.[28] Exceptions to this general rule do occur when public or media interest is aroused by highly innovative, experimental, or controversial programs. Then participation in the implementation process can have important public relations value for policymakers, demonstrating responsiveness to constituents' concerns.

The involvement of policymakers in the implementation process is also more likely when there is opportunity for bureaucrats to write rules and regulations in such a way that the legislative intent of a policy might not be met. Civil servants may seize the opportunity, when presented with loosely written legislation, to bias implementation towards goals not intended or foreseen by policymakers.[29] In these cases, politicians may fear that voters will attribute the failure of a program to inadequate policy, rather than to the implementation process; thus they may take an active role in attempting to guide program implementors.

Finally, when a piece of legislation is controversial or innovative, policymakers are likely to have varying recollections of legislative intent, depending on their political persuasions, the length of time since passage, and the nature of intervening events. They may attempt to actively intervene in the implementation process in order to guard against "corruption" of "their" program.

In AHCCCS, key policymakers at the county, state, and federal levels cooperatively developed and solicited support for the more innovative aspects of the program, including the concept of competitive bidding by providers. All participants were alert to the potential for "corruption" of the legislative intent during implementation, since this could anger those constituents and interest groups whose support was necessary for development of the program. In part due to the perceived high level of political risk associated with any experimental program, as well as the program's high level of media visibility, legislators formalized a mechanism for involvement in implementation: the Joint Legislative Health Care Cost Containment Committee (or Joint Legislative Oversight Committee, JLOC). JLOC activities during the implementation period were directed at assuring that the legislative intent of the AHCCCS legislation was not seriously modified in the preparation of rules and regulations by the AHCCCS Division. With regard to details of the competitive bidding process, however, the AHCCCS legislation was vague. One role of liaison staff between policymakers and implementors on this issue was, therefore, to discover that intent and to reconcile it with other pressures faced by the implementors.

As the existence of the JLOC demonstrates, the traditional lack of attention displayed by policymakers towards implementation issues did not characterize AHCCCS. Press attention increased the interest of constituents and pressure groups, and consequently the interest of politicians, in the implementation process. The lack of specific guidance in the legislation concerning competitive bidding led to ongoing interaction between legislators and implementors, which generated conflict and created confusion.

Multiple Decision Points. In their study of the implementation of an employment project, Pressman and Wildavsky note that the number of decision points where consensus from the participants is needed is often far greater than anticipated, ultimately causing implementation failure.[30] They suggest that legislators, when designing programs, minimize the number of implementation decision points open to political pressure. However, legislators may not always find this suggestion attractive, since multiple decision points sometimes can serve important political objectives.[31]

The presence of "multiple decision points" did, in fact, create significant problems in the implementation of the competitive bidding process in AHCCCS. Because of the experimental nature of the program, many important decisions concerning the bidding process were relegated to the implementation period. To make these decisions, it was necessary that interaction occur among federal representatives of HCFA and DHHS Region IX offices, members and staff of the JLOC, the governor and his staff, Arizona Department of Health Services personnel, personnel in other bureaus within state government (Risk

Management, Attorney General, and Administration, in particular), AHCCCS Division staff, and MSGI staff. Facilitating this interaction placed considerable strain on staff resources and delayed decision making on important questions relating to bidding design and bid evaluation.

Federalism. Federalism, and particularly the federal government's control over funds, is blamed by a number of researchers as one of the major politically based causes of implementation failure.[32] Arizona policymakers attempted to circumvent "federalism problems" in the design of AHCCCS. They perceived a lack of federal responsiveness to, and awareness of, local needs in the Medicaid program, and did not wish their program to be subordinated to federal officials. Many local lawmakers had developed reputations and strong constituencies based on their opposition to federal mandates and the requirements that often accompany federal funding of local programs. As a research and demonstration program, AHCCCS was funded under Title XIX through federal approval of waivers, which removed many of the requirements included in traditional Medicaid programs. While oversight was required in that HCFA had to approve waiver requests, the usual conflict between federal and local officials was minimized by reducing interaction over enforcement of most rules. Thus, AHCCCS is viewed by local voters and implementors as a state-developed and managed program.

Characteristics of Bureaucracies

The structure and operating methods of public agencies can sometimes impede successful policy implementation.[33] Elmore states that the unresponsiveness of large public bureaucracies to new policy initiatives is more often than not attributable to failure to connect "the big ideas" of policymakers with the "mundane coping mechanisms of implementors."[34] The fact that agency personnel and leadership rarely have roles in formulating policy and, therefore, have little stake in the ultimate success or failure of a program also mitigates against efforts to improve the implementation process.[35] The disposition, or attitude, of implementors towards the policy to be implemented is crucial, in that personal motivation towards a program can either expedite or hinder implementation. Communication within and between agencies responsible for implementation also is essential for implementation to proceed in a timely, consistent way.

Organizational Factors. Many problems in implementation have been attributed to two characteristics of bureaucratic organizations: standard operating procedures (SOPs) and fragmentation. SOPs can be useful in overburdened bureaucracies, since they provide a uniform, economical way of dealing with multiple decisions and changes in personnel. However, SOPs also may function as obstacles to the implementation of new programs by inhibiting change, delaying progress, and causing undesirable actions.[36] Fragmentation often arises when public programs are multidimensional and require the expertise and input of multiple organizations within government.[37] The assignment of responsibility to multiple units can slow transmissions of information and create situations where gaps or overlaps in responsibility arise. Fragmentation can also result in competition for resources and related power between agencies, and even strong, unilateral direction from top policymakers may not be sufficient to overcome this problem.[38]

Pressman and Wildavsky, and Mead offer potential solutions to implementation problems caused by overreliance on SOPs and by fragmentation within public bureaucracies.[39] They suggest that the establishment of a new organization or the "rebirth" of an organization as a new bureau within an existing department can be useful in bypassing the usual SOPs and routines that occur in existing organizations. Fragmentation may be reduced through merger of separate program functions into "umbrella agencies."

Arizona policymakers anticipated the difficulties that might arise if AHCCCS were implemented by an existing agency within state government. Consequently, they mandated the formation of a new and separate division within the Department of Health Services, with the sole responsibility of implementing the AHCCCS. Since the AHCCCS legislation contained only a minimal description of the competitive bidding process, AHCCCS Division staff probably saw significant potential for "policymaking" during implementation, thus increasing their "stake" in the program. Also, lawmakers used competitive bidding to hire a private contract administrator with substantial program responsibilities. By contracting with a private organization, state legislators hoped to avoid the development of a large, new state agency (which would be difficult to dismantle subsequently) and to secure staff who were not overly influenced by traditional Medicaid programs.

While the use of SOPs within the AHCCCS Division and MSGI was discouraged by the fact that both organizations were new, they continued to play a role in the decision-making process of agencies playing collaborative implementation roles. For example, the process of obtaining reinsurance for providers was intended to be complete prior to July 1982 so that bidders would not include the costs of reinsurance in their bids. Also, implementors did not want small provider organizations to avoid involvement in AHCCCS due to fear of large claims not covered by reinsurance. However, the Risk Management Division within Arizona state government applied existing SOPs to reinsurance acquisition by the program, and this resulted in a failure to obtain reinsurance before providers submitted bids. Potential bidders did not have confidence that the reinsurance problem would be solved by the program startup date and may have submitted higher bids as a result.

While the creation of new administrative organizations may have minimized the role of SOPs in program implementation, it introduced considerable fragmentation. In implementing the competitive bidding system, the transfer of responsibility from the AHCCCS Division to MSGI occurred just as efforts to establish the service delivery network were initiated (June 1982). Much of the work done by the state Division in the conceptualization and exploration of potential bidding mechanisms was seemingly lost, or at least underutilized, due to this transfer of responsibility. The involvement of two separate agencies in designing and implementing the bidding process resulted in the predictable duplication of efforts and bureaucratic functions and the diversion of resources towards the drafting of numerous "transmittal memos" flowing between the organizations.

Fragmentation also was evident in the involvement of the JLOC and the attorney general in the numerous aspects of the competitive bidding process. A lack of communication between bureaucratic units precluded early warning that one crucial design element being considered by the AHCCCS Division director and staff—direct negotiation over price—was illegal under existing state law. While environmental pressures increased concern by AHCCCS Division and MSGI staff that bid levels might exceed what they considered to be the "actuarily sound price," they chose to await the results of the bidding before addressing this problem. A critical meeting in August 1982 brought together key legislative leadership, AHCCCS Division director and staff, MSGI staff, and the attorney general to decide on how to deal with the "high" bid prices submitted in six of Arizona's 14 counties. Apparently, it was not until this meeting, barely two weeks before those clients declared eligible were to begin enrollment in health plans, that the illegality of direct price negotiation with bidders was clearly conveyed to program administrators. Only a last-minute agreement between the attorney general, the JLOC, and the Division director to request "voluntary price reductions" by bidders, according to a defined set of criteria, allowed completion of the bidding process. Had this accord not been reached, the bidding process presumably would have been repeated, delaying the operational date for the program.

Dispositions of Implementors. While successful policy implementation depends partly on the design of the program to be implemented and the structure of the bureaucracy responsible for implementation, the attitudes of implementors within responsible agencies are also important determinants of success or failure.[40] In cases where bureaucrats differ significantly from policymakers in their attitudes, it is difficult for policymakers to change the dispositions of implementors, nor is it usually possible, given civil service regulations, to remove those opposed to a specific policy. Negative attitudes of implementors towards public policies can cause delays in implementation, a lack of enforcement of policies, or poor compliance with legislative intent. Implementors sometimes have strong positive attitudes towards policies, often in association with the establishment of innovative programs. Described by Rourke as "organizational esprit," such enthusiasm can maintain the interest of the talented personnel necessary to successfully implement a complex program.[41]

The hiring of AHCCCS staff with intellectual and career involvement in the substantive aspects of the legislation facilitated implementation. AHCCCS Division staff, in particular, demonstrated intellectual commitment towards the program beyond the norm in public bureaucracies. Furthermore, the legislation's lack of guidelines for design of the competitive bidding system resulted in increased discretion for implementors and, along with the sense of urgency all participants felt, contributed to the development of a supportive, "organizational esprit," which facilitated implementation.

Communication. Communication within and between public agencies and legislators can be a critical factor for effective implementation. According to Van Meter and Van Horn, the "clarity of standards and objectives, the accuracy of their communication to implementors, and the consistency (or uniformity) with which they are communicated by various sources of information" are all important factors in implementing programs.[42] For instance, "bare bones legislation" can inadequately communicate legislative intent to implementors and require ongoing communication between legislators and implementors during the implementation process. The accuracy and adequacy of transmission of information among participants in the implementation process often depends on the existence of well-established communication channels.[43] Furthermore, it is important that lower organizational levels provide effective feedback to decision makers so that implementation decisions are based on current and accurate information.

Poor communication between levels and agencies of the state and federal bureaucracy hindered the implementation of AHCCCS. Many of the examples cited previously support this conclusion. For instance, the confusion over the legality of price negotiation with bidders might never have occurred if the implications of existing state procurement statutes, which include precedent on state bidding for contracts, had been clearly communicated to program legislators and administrators. However, no consistent channel of communication concerning the program existed between the attorney general's office and legislative committees or executive agencies. This resulted in ongoing controversy over the legality of various provisions of the legislation and the ensuing rules and regulations, particularly as they pertained to competitive bidding.

Summary

Implementation of the Arizona bidding process was complex, raised difficult-to-resolve issues, and was influenced by many of the same factors that previous authors have identified as important for program implementation. The resources, including time, available for program implementation were extremely limited. This restricted the attention that could be devoted to issues of bidding design, constrained the technical assistance that could be offered to providers, delayed the development of program rules and regulations and criteria for selection of winning bidders, and, as a consequence, created confusion and uncertainty among potential bidders during the initial stages of the implementation process (see chapter 7). These problems were compounded by the multiple decision points and fragmentation of authority and responsibility built into the design of the program and contributed to communication breakdowns among agencies involved in program implementation.

Despite the efforts of an uncommonly dedicated group of program implementors, external pressures, resource limitations, and features of program design led to the implementation of a bidding system with weaker cost containment incentives than were probably envisioned by its supporters. This result is primarily due to two strategies adopted in the implementation process. First, the award of contracts to multiple full service bidders in as many counties as possible reduced provider incentives to submit low bids. Second, as suggested in chapter 4, the adoption of a "pseudonegotiation" process in response to initial bids reduced the incentives for bidders to compete on the basis of price.[44] The implementation process also illustrated the political liabilities, previously discussed in chapter 4, in competitive bidding systems as applied to indigent medical care.

Notes

1. For an extensive bibliography of the literature pertaining to competitive bidding in general, see M. Starke, "Competitive Bidding: A Comprehensive Bibliography," *Operations Research* 19 (March-April 1971): 484–90.
2. S. M. Shortell and M. A. Solomon, "Improving Health Care Policy Research," *Journal of Health Politics, Policy, and Law* 6 (Winter 1982): 689.
3. The "implementation period" itself is defined in a variety of ways by different authors. For the purposes of this chapter we adopt the approaches taken by Van Meter and Van Horn and by Schneider. Van Meter and Van Horn state that "policy implementation encompasses those actions by public and private individuals (or groups) that are directed at the achievement of objectives set forth in prior policy decisions." See D. S. Van Meter and C. E. Van Horn, "The Policy Implementation Process: A Conceptual Framework," *Administration and Society* 6 (February 1975): 462. Schneider decomposes the implementation process into a "planning" phase that occurs immediately following policy adoption and includes acquisition of necessary resources and completion of tasks necessary to develop an institution capable of carrying out the implementation process; a "start-up" phase that includes the first performance of tasks; and "fine tuning" that transforms new procedures to routine operations. The implementation period examined in this analysis consists of the "planning" phase and the "start-up" phase described by Schneider. See A. L. Schneider, "Studying Policy Implementation—A Conceptual Framework," *Evaluation Review* 6 (December 1972): 715–30.
4. Van Meter and Van Horn, "Policy Implementation Process;" L. M. Mead, *Institutional Analysis: An Approach to Implementation Problems in*

Medicaid (Washington, D.C.: The Urban Institute, April 1977); E. C. Hargrove, *The Missing Link: The Study of the Implementation of Social Policy* (Washington, D.C.: The Urban Institute, July 1975); G. C. Edwards III, *Implementing Public Policy* (Washington, D.C.: Congressional Quarterly Press, Inc., 1980); F. E. Rourke, *Bureaucracy, Politics and Public Policy* (Boston: Little, Brown and Co., 1976).

5. Van Meter and Van Horn, "Policy Implementation Process," p. 462.
6. Mead, *Institutional Analysis*, p. 49.
7. Hargrove, *Missing Link*.
8. Edwards, *Implementing Public Policy*.
9. Rourke, *Bureaucracy*.
10. R. K. Yin, "Studying the Implementation of Public Programs," in W. Williams and R. F. Elmore, eds., *Social Program Implementation* (New York: Academic Press, 1976), p. 39.
11. Initial provider interviews were concentrated in the period after submission of bids but before the selection of winning bidders. This schedule was designed to minimize the potential influence of the research on bidding behavior, while avoiding interview responses colored by results of the bidding. Interviews with others were conducted throughout the implementation process to capture the perceptions of key actors at various points in time. The authors did not participate formally or informally in the implementation process, nor did they have any prior expectations concerning the manner in which the bidding system would be implemented.
12. Mead, *Insititutional Analysis*.
13. Hargrove, *Missing Link*.
14. Rourke, *Bureaucracy*, p. 173.
15. S. Williams, *Arizona Daily Star*, September 17, 1982.
16. K. Pfitzer, *Tucson Citizen*, June 25, 1982.
17. C. McClain, *Tucson Citizen*, July 27, 1982.
18. See Hargrove, *Missing Link;* Mead, *Institutional Analysis;* J. L. Pressman and Aaron Wildavsky, *Implementation: How Great Expectations in Washington Are Dashed in Oakland* (Berkeley: University of California Press, 1973).
19. Edwards, *Implementing Public Policy*.
20. In fact, there were substantial cost overruns for the contract to MSGI, and these overruns required additional state appropriations. It is not clear why state officials chose to fund the overruns rather than contest them during the first year of the program. Certainly there was a concern for continuity in program administration, as well as a recognition that changing program requirements necessitated some additional expenses by MSGI. During the second year of the program, MSGI was dismissed as administrator and its contract is currently the subject of litigation. Whatever the circumstances of these cost overruns, they did reinforce the need for the bidding system to demonstrate "visible" cost savings.

21. The confusion caused by division of responsibilities is discussed at greater length in the subsequent section on bureaucratic factors affecting implementation.

22. Edwards, *Implementing Public Policy*, defines authority as the ability either to "give" funds, staff, or technical assistance or to "constrain" agencies through withdrawal of funds, issuing of subpoenas, taxation, or other sanctions. Van Meter and Van Horn, "Policy Implementation Process," classify authority or enforcement activities between governments or organizations as either technical assistance or positive and negative sanctions and indicate that while the use of coercive powers is not desirable, those responsible for implementation must nevertheless have the authority to use "action-forcing mechanisms" to require compliance or prevent counterproductive behavior.

23. "Firm Managing ACCESS Faces 2-Pronged Probe," *Tucson Citizen*, February 10, 1983; J. Nelsson, "Babbitt Assigns Aide to Key Health-System Post," *Arizona Republic*, February 11, 1983.

24. For a discussion of the incentives implicit in different bidding systems for indigent care, see chapter 4.

25. Pressman and Wildavsky, *Implementation*.

26. Hargrove, *Missing Link*, p. 69.

27. As explained by Williams, those responsible for the formulation of policy are oriented towards the "policy sphere" while implementors are oriented towards the "operations sphere," where programs are implemented and administered and where services are delivered. Neither group of actors is particularly effective in controlling the functioning of the "opposite" sphere, resulting in frustration, particularly among policymakers when programs do not meet established goals. See W. Williams, "Implementation Problems in Federally Funded Programs," in W. Williams and R. F. Elmore, eds., *Social Program Implementation* (New York: Academic Press, 1976), p. 1542.

28. Hargrove, *Missing Link*, p. 33.

29. Ibid.

30. Pressman and Wildavsky, *Implementation*.

31. Mead, *Institutional Analysis*.

32. For instance, Pressman and Wildavsky, *Implementation*, liken federal funds to "internal foreign aid." They conclude that federal policymakers often do not perceive the political realities of implementing federally funded programs at the local level. These realities differ from one location to another, and overlooking them can lead to a rocky transition from policymaking to service delivery for program implementors. This issue is also discussed at length by M. Derthick, *New Towns In Town* (Washington, D.C.: The Urban Institute, 1972). Derthick's study provides an example where federal and local goals and perceptions were diametrically opposed. Federal officials wanted to use what they considered to be "cheap" land within several cities to establish new, racially

integrated urban communities. They lacked an awareness of local laws that prohibited sales of the land at the prices they had envisioned, local opposition to the use of the land in a way that would generate minimal tax revenues, and local leaders' fears of pushing racially mixed communities on reluctant constituents. In addition, federal officials lacked power to enforce local participation.

33. Williams, "Implementation Problems," observes that the usual orientation of public agencies is "down toward the place of service delivery," rather than "up toward where policies are made."

34. R. F. Elmore, "Organizational Models of Social Program Implementation," *Public Policy* 26 (Spring 1978), p. 208.

35. Hargrove, *Missing Link.*

36. Edwards, *Implementing Public Policy*, p. 125, states that SOPs "develop as internal responses to the limited time and resources of implementors and the desire for uniformity in the operation of complex and widely dispersed organizations," and that they often remain in effect due to inertia. Mead, *Institutional Analysis*, p. 121, cites "the development of inertia around established administrative routines" as an explanation for the mobility of federal and state administrators to implement innovations within Medicaid. He points to delays in implementing the EPSDT program and in utilizing automated claims mechanisms as examples of bureaucratic inertia, and blames the presence of personnel left over from earlier, less complex health and welfare programs for the use of established routines or SOPs that were inappropriate.

37. Edwards, *Implementing Public Policy*, p. 134, defines fragmentation as "the dispersion of responsibility of a policy area among several organizational units."

38. Mead, *Institutional Analysis*, attributes some of the implementation problems in the Medicaid program to what he terms "division among bureaucracies," or fragmentation. He observes that "each bureau, in its own self interest, commits more resources to defending its turf against the incursions of other bureaus than is rational from an overall, social point of view" (p. 122). As a result, Edwards, *Implementing Public Policy*, states that "the more actors and agencies involved in a particular policy and the more interdependent their decisions, the less the probability of successful implementation" (p. 134). Clearly, the problems caused by "fragmentation" are identified with those of "limited authority" and "multiple decision points."

39. Pressman and Wildavsky, *Implementation;* Mead, *Institutional Analysis.*

40. Van Meter and Van Horn, "Policy Implementation Process," specify three elements of implementor's responses that determine the likelihood of support or rejection of a policy: a) cognition, comprehension, or understanding; b) direction of the response (acceptance, rejection, or neutrality); and c) the intensity of the response. Edwards, *Implementing Public Policy*, observes that the majority of public policies fall into the implementor's

"zone of indifference," where the reaction is neutral and where policy is likely to be implemented in a fairly straightforward manner.

41. However, Rourke, *Bureaucracy*, also observes that "it is possible to discern within bureaucratic organizations themselves a tendency to move from an initial period of enthusiasm and energy to a subsequent stage when the organization becomes routinized and gradually loses a good deal of its original elan" (p. 92). He suggests that efforts be made to take advantage of early "youthful zeal" to undertake the bulk of difficult implementation activities before SOPs or "administrative arteriosclerosis" begin to appear.

42. Van Meter and Van Horn, "Policy Implementation Process," p. 466.

43. Mead, *Institutional Analysis*, states that "viewed from the top, the communication problem is that the leaders cannot generate signals clear or strong enough to reach the bottom levels reliably, nor can they receive back adequate information from there" (p. 116).

44. Experimental studies of competitive bidding indicate that, just as in a competitive market, participants in a bidding system learn how to participate more effectively over time. Thus, prices as determined in an 'initial' round of bidding may not reflect long-run prices and therefore may not provide an accurate indication of the cost containment potential of the bidding process. See, for instance, Gary J. Miller and Charles R. Platt, "Revenue Generating Properties of Sealed Bid Auctions: An Experimental Analysis of One-Price and Discriminative Processes," in V. L. Smith, ed., *Research in Experimental Economics, Vol. 3* (Greenwich, Connecticut: JAI Press, 1983).

7

Provider Participation in the First Round of Bidding for Arizona's Indigent Patients

A major concern during the implementation of the competitive bidding process in Arizona was the degree to which providers would choose to participate in the program and the strategies they would employ in constructing their bids. The ideal competitive bidding process for indigent medical care would involve multiple, high quality providers competing for patients aggressively on price. However, the likelihood that providers will "play the game" in this manner depends on complex considerations that will vary in importance across type of provider, bidding rules, market conditions, and the actions of program managers. The first part of this chapter provides a conceptual framework for viewing provider decision making. The uncertainty involved in the bidding process, the characteristics of the possible payoffs for providers, and the multiperiod nature of the bidding environment are identified as key elements in the formulation of bidding strategies. This conceptual framework is then applied to a discussion of the bidding strategies employed by four different types of bidders in the first round of bidding in the Arizona experi-

The majority of this chapter was published previously in the Summer 1984 issue of *Inquiry*. It is used with permission of the Blue Cross and Blue Shield Association. © 1984 Blue Cross and Blue Shield Association. All rights reserved.

ment. The chapter concludes by discussing state actions that could reduce the uncertainty facing providers in the bidding process.

A Conceptual Framework for
Provider Bidding Behavior

In his summary of the literature, Engelbrecht-Wiggans (1980) characterizes bidding processes as "games with incomplete information."[1] One aspect of the game is the "true state of nature" that, for an indigent medical care auction, includes service utilization per indigent, the cost of delivering services, the number of indigents, the objectives of the participating bidders, the number of bidders, and the rules for allocating program eligibles to winning bidders. In most conceptualizations of bidding processes, it is assumed that bidders know the possible values for all of these items, but not the particular values that will be observed in a specific situation. However, each bidder has some information available to assess the state of nature. For instance, a provider may have some experience delivering care to a particular group of indigents and can use this information to predict per capita utilization of services by indigents in a given area.[2]

Each bidding process also has a "payoff function" that determines the reward to the winning bidders. While the payoff function is known to all bidders, the actual payoff is not known precisely since it depends on such uncertain factors as the unit costs of providing services, the utilization of services, and the number of indigents under contract. Therefore, there is a distribution of possible payoffs associated with each bid at the time the bid is submitted.

Finally, most competitive bidding processes are repetitive in nature. For instance, competitive bidding in indigent medical care programs is likely to result in one- or two-year contracts with the state, with subsequent rebidding. This complicates the provider's decision problem, since the future impact of bids submitted in any given round of bidding must also be taken into account when developing bidding strategy.

The conceptual framework that follows is useful in understanding the bidding strategies that might be adopted by providers in "playing the game." The framework is developed first with two simplifying assumptions: (1) in constructing bids, providers are concerned only with maximizing their profits from indigent program enrollees and (2) the "time horizon" for bidder decision making does not exceed the length of the initial contract. This allows the discussion to focus initially on the choices and uncertainties inherent in the bidding problem. Then the conceptual framework is broadened by discussing the implications for provider bidding behavior of relaxing each of these assumptions.

A Simplified Provider Bidding Problem

When bidding for indigent medical care contracts, the provider is likely to be confronted with three situations requiring explicit decisions: (1) whether or not to complete the research necessary to prepare a bid; (2) if the research is completed, the features to incorporate in a bid; and (3) if negotiation is required, the strategy to use in negotiating with the state. In addition to these decision points in the bidding process, there are several uncertain events that can influence the final outcome, or payoff, associated with a particular bid. The sequence of decisions and events in a simplified bidding process is presented in decision tree form in figure 7.1, with definitions in table 7.1.[3]

The Research Decision. The first decision for the potential bidder is whether to invest time and resources in doing the research required to bid.[4] A decision not to invest in bid preparation is equivalent to a decision not to bid, since the requirements of bidding typically include a substantial amount of documentation available only through some sort of research effort. The purpose of the research involved in bid preparation is primarily to construct per indigent per month cost estimates, which are the basis for formulating bid prices and for calculating payoffs. The possible cost estimates resulting from the research process are assumed to be known to the provider, but the research identifies the particular estimate that seems most probable for the bidding situation. For illustrative purposes, only three possible cost estimates are shown in figure 7.1.

Providers might decide not to invest in research if, for example, they view bidding as "prohibitively expensive," or they believe that the criteria for selecting winning bidders are "stacked against them." On the other hand, they may decide to invest in research and subsequently to submit a bid even if they have strong prior beliefs that they will not profit from an indigent contract. In this case, providers may be motivated by fear of the uncertain consequences of not participating. A decision to invest in research may "buy time" to evaluate these consequences.

Figure 7.1 Decision Tree for Bidding on Indigent Medical Care Contracts

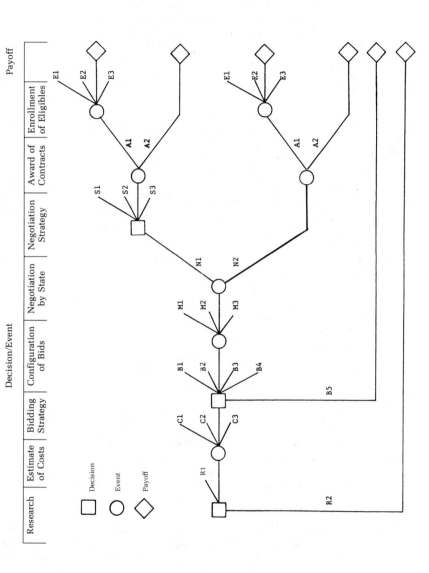

Table 7.1   The Decision-Event Chain in Competitive Bidding for Indigent Medical Care

---

1. Decision: Conduct research necessary to prepare a bid
   a. Yes (R1) The option to submit a bid is preserved
   b. No (R2) Provider cannot participate in the bidding process

2. Event: Projections of per indigent costs resulting from research
   a. High cost estimate (C1)
   b. Medium cost estimate (C2)
   c. Low cost estimate (C3)

3. Decision: Determine features of bid
   a. High price, high capacity (B1)
   b. High price, low capacity (B2)
   c. Low price, high capacity (B3)
   d. Low price, low capacity (B4)
   e. No bid submitted (B5)

4. Event: Configuration of submitted bids
   a. B3 bids dominate, there are many bidders (M1)
   b. Mixture of bids, average number of bidders (M2)
   c. B2 bids dominate, there are few bidders (M3)

5. Event: State negotiates over bids
   a. State institutes negotiation process (N1)
   b. State accepts bids without negotiation (N2)

6. Decision: Determine negotiation strategy
   a. Offer large reduction in price (S1)
   b. Offer small reduction in price (S2)
   c. Do not reduce price (S3)

7. Event: Contracts are awarded by state
   a. Selected as a winning bidder (A1)
   b. Not selected as a winning bidder (A2)

8. Event: Enrollment of program eligibles
   a. Enrollment attains or closely approaches specified capacity (E1)
   b. Enrollment exceeds half of specified capacity (E2)
   c. Enrollment is less than half of specified capacity (E3)

9. Payoff: Difference between provider revenues and costs attributable to the program during the contract period covered by the bidding process

---

The Construction of the Bid. Any bid is inevitably a mix of price and nonprice features, and potential bidders must first decide which mix to build into a bid.[5] In this simplified descriptive framework, it will be assumed that all bidders meet minimum standards of organizational soundness and medical care quality, and that the state places no weight on exceeding these standards. Therefore, the only nonprice variable is the maximum number of indigents a bidder is willing to serve. The upper capacity limit is known to the bidder in advance of bidding and is equal to the state's estimate of the number of program eligibles in the geographic area over which the bid is defined. The number of indigents actually served by the bidder does not necessarily equal the number requested but depends on how many winning bidders are selected by the state, the maximum capacities specified by other winners, and the process by which program eligibles enroll in, or are assigned by the state to, winning health care plans. In addition to specifying a capacity, each bid must contain a price per enrollee per month. A provider's bid price will reflect such considerations as estimated costs, desired profits per indigent, expected number and bid prices of competitors, and the probability that negotiation with the state will be required.[6] While the number of possible combinations of bid price and capacity is infinite in theory, only four bid categories are defined in table 7.1, along with a "no bid" option (B5). It is assumed that the state has a preference ordering over bids, all else equal, as follows: B3 > B4 > B2 > B1.[7]

The first uncertain event after the provider submits a bid is the overall configuration of the bids submitted, which depends on the behavior of competitors. The second uncertain event is the state's negotiation policy. The state's decision to negotiate after bids are submitted will depend on the provider's bid and the general configuration of bids but is uncertain from the provider's point of view. The state could decide to request a bid price reduction if a provider submitted a high bid and the other bids were also high. On the other hand, the state could choose not to negotiate with a high bidder if the other bids were low and the capacity offered by the bidder were not needed to guarantee that all indigents were served.

The Negotiation Strategy. If the state initiates a negotiation process, the bidder must determine a negotiation strategy. One option is to refuse to lower the submitted bid price. Figure 7.1 also illustrates two other possible decisions corresponding to large and small price reductions. After the negotiation process, or the state's decision not to negotiate, a third uncertain event occurs: contracts are awarded. The probability that a provider is selected as a winning bidder depends on the characteristics of the provider's bid, the characteristics of other bids, the state's decision to negotiate, and the provider's negotiation strategy. Clearly a provider who submits a low price, high capacity bid (B3) when other bidders offer high prices and low capacities (M3), and then reduces the bid through negotiation (S2) has a better chance of being selected than a provider with a high bid price (B2) in a competitive market (M1) who refuses to negotiate (S3).

Finally, the division of program eligibles among winning bidders is the fourth uncertain event from the providers' point of view at the time bids are submitted. The actions of the program administrators in offering eligibles an enrollment option or assigning them to plans will differ depending on the bid prices submitted by all providers, the responsiveness of providers to negotiation, and the provider's own bid. Program administrators can have a major effect on provider profits if they choose to allocate at least some indigents to winning bidders. The process they adopt can determine how quickly winning providers reach their enrollment goals, as well as the characteristics of patients enrolled with specific providers, and consequently the payoff providers receive from the program. Program officials can also affect the revenues of providers who are not winning bidders through their policies for reimbursement of care provided to indigents outside of the contract-provider delivery system (either before or after the enrollment of these indigents with a winning provider) and the restrictions they impose on the use of noncontract providers for emergency care.

Estimating the Payoff. The bidder's decision problem at the time of bid submission is to select the bid that maximizes the expected value of the difference between revenues and costs. In theory, this requires assigning subjective probabilities to each uncertain event and calculating the expected payoff associated with each possible "pathway" through the decision tree in figure 7.1. Based on these subjective estimates, the decision maker can "roll back" the decision tree to assign an expected payoff value to each possible bid and to a decision to submit no bid.[8] In some circumstances, there may be no bid that yields a positive expected payoff. However, the projected losses associated with not bidding may exceed the losses associated with at least one bid, leading the provider to "play the game" by submitting a bid even when a negative payoff is expected.

Even though actions and uncertain events that are in reality continuous variables are depicted as discrete categories in figure 7.1, a great deal of effort and resources obviously would be necessary to accurately estimate payoffs for all of the pathways implied by the decision tree. Therefore, potential bidders may choose to eliminate whole sets of pathways by making simplifying assumptions about uncertain events or by adopting decision rules that limit the set of acceptable payoff functions.[9]

The Provider's Objective Function

It is likely that the objectives of providers are considerably more complex than maximizing the difference between the revenues and costs of providing care to indigents. For example, the number of indigents served by the provider could affect the provider's ability to attract nonindigent patients. Or the bid price submitted in the competitive bidding process might affect the levels of reimbursements from other payers. The following statement of the expected payoff (PF) from the submission of a given bid, B, for indigent patient contracts accommodates these possibilities.[10]

$$E(PF \mid B) = E[(IP + NIP) \mid B] - K \qquad (1)$$
$$IP = n (BP - C) \qquad (2)$$
$$NIP = F(BP, n) \qquad (3)$$

Equation 1 states that the expected payoff from bid B is the sum of the bidder's expected profits from serving both indigents and nonindigents, minus the costs of bid preparation (K). Indigent profits (equation 2) are equal to the bid price (BP) minus costs (C) per enrollee month times the number of enrollee months (n), such that n/12 is less than or equal to the bidder's capacity as specified in the bid. Profits derived from providing care to nonindigents (NIP) can be affected by the bid price at which indigents are provided care, as well as the number of indigents served. The exact nature of this relationship will vary with the type of bidding organization (as is evident in the following discussion of Arizona bidders). For instance, if an HMO enrolls large numbers of indigents it may become less attractive to members of employed groups. Conversely, in other circumstances a contract to serve indigents could have a positive effect on other profit sources. A rural hospital, for instance, may find that the increased revenues and occupancy rates that result from winning a contract allow it to expand the range of services it offers and thereby attract more medical staff and admissions. Whatever the direction of these "indirect impacts" of contract awards on expected profits, the bidding organization must attempt to evaluate them accurately before bidding, as they will influence the payoff from bidding.

The formulation of bidding strategy becomes still more complex if expectations concerning the number of individuals who will be served under contract are not independent of the bid price. This can occur, for example, if the state assigns to the organizations submitting the lowest bids those eligibles who do not exercise a choice among available providers. Given this policy, low bids are now more attractive since they contribute to expected profits in two ways: by increasing the probability of being awarded a contract and by increasing the number of individuals to whom services are delivered if the contract is secured.

Capacity limitations specified as part of a bid can limit the potential magnitude of an adverse indirect impact by setting the maximum capacity figure at a relatively low level. This is illustrated in figure 7.2, a hypothetical relationship between maximum capacity level and net expected profits from a contract. When the specified capacity is low, enrollment is likely to match capacity limitations, since at least that number of indigents in the enrollment pool will select the organization as their preferred health care provider. However, as the capacity limitation increases, the potential for actual enrollment to fall below specified capacity also increases. This accounts for the positive, but declining, effect of the increase in bid capacity on the direct profits from an indigent contract. To obtain the marginal addition to the organization's profits that would occur under the indigent contract, the bidder would need to consider indirect effects, such as expected losses (if any) on profits from private group contracts. If relatively few indigents are covered by the contract, the expected effect on private group profits is minimal. However, as the number of indigent enrollees increases, the negative impact on the enrollment of private groups also could increase. When this impact is taken into account, the expected profit from the contract may be related to bid capacity in the manner depicted in figure 7.2. The maximum point on the "expected profits" curve determines the capacity the bidder should specify in submitting a bid.

The expected value of the payoff from a bid is equal to the weighted average of all possible payoffs (IP plus NIP) associated with the initial bid, B, where the weights are the probabilities that each specific payoff will occur, given B. While one criteria for constructing a bid is to choose that bid which maximizes (PF|B), this decision rule for providers may lack realism when the bidding decision could have a substantial impact on the overall finances of the bidder. In this case, some bidders might consider the variation of possible payoffs, as well as their expected value, to be an important part of their objective functions.

Markowitz (1952) noted this tendency in the decision making of firms, and defined an efficient decision as one in which the standard deviation of the payoff is minimized for a given expected value or,

Figure 7.2   Hypothetical Relationship between Expected Profits and Bid Capacity Limitation for an Indigent Contract

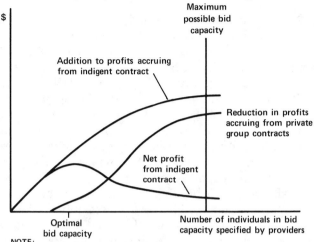

NOTE:
This figure is constructed for a specific bid price.
A different set of relationships would apply to each possible bid price.

alternatively, the expected value of the payoff is maximized for a given standard deviation.[11] Faced with this trade-off, different providers may adopt different rules of thumb that limit the relevant decisions to a subset of efficient points. For instance, they may:[12]

1. Maximize expected payoff subject to an upper bound on the standard deviation.
2. Minimize the standard deviation of the payoff subject to a lower bound on the expected payoff.
3. Maximize the expected payoff subject to some limitation on the probability of disaster (say, bankruptcy).
4. Minimize the probability of disaster, subject to a lower bound on the payoff.

Providers who incorporate these considerations in their decision making are likely to submit different bids than providers who simply attempt to maximize the expected payoff from bidding.

Considerations in Repetitive Bidding

Further realism can be added to the conceptual framework by acknowledging that bidding on indigent medical care is likely to be repetitive. When bidding occurs on a regular basis, the objective of the bidder is not simply to maximize expected profit subject to risk constraints (or some similar objective function) in the first round of bidding, but over the entire expected life of the bidding process. Furthermore, decisions and events in initial rounds of bidding could influence the subjective estimates of probabilities and payoffs made in subsequent rounds. For instance, suppose that provider A, with low costs, submitted a high price, high capacity (B1) bid, found an uncompetitive market, did not lower the bid during negotiation, was selected as a winning bidder, and was favored in the allocation of patients by the state, earning a handsome profit. This favorable experience could result in different subjective probability estimates for the second round than those of provider B, who followed a different path to the second round of bidding.

The evaluation of the bidding process for indigent medical care over time can be characterized in three phases: initial, experimental, and institutional. The initial phase is the first round of bidding. There are no incumbent bidders, and a great deal of uncertainty exists with respect to the characteristics of the true state of nature and the behavior of competitors. Information is expensive to acquire and potential payoffs are difficult to estimate. In the experimental phase, beginning with round two, there are incumbent bidders, information is cheaper to obtain, the behavior of competitors is more predictable, and payoffs become easier to estimate. However, uncertainty still exists due to changes in bidding rules and program regulations. The experimental phase moves into the institutional phase as program procedures become more stable. The institutional phase is characterized by much less uncertainty for the bidders and consequently less variation in their bidding behavior from year to year. Contracts may be awarded for longer time periods and may be subject to renewal without competitive rebidding. The problem that providers face is to bid in the initial phase in a way that maximizes expected returns from indigents and private patients over all three phases, subject to acceptable levels of risk.[13] Since pathways and outcomes from each phase affect decisions in the subsequent phase, the repetitive nature of bidding escalates the complexity of provider decision making.

Conclusion

This conceptual framework for viewing the provider's decision problem in bidding on indigent medical care contracts suggests that bidders are confronted with great uncertainty, must utilize unreliable information to make decisions, have complicated objectives, and face complex bidding environments. The remainder of this chapter will utilize the framework in an analysis of the experience of different providers participating in the Arizona bidding process.

Provider Bidding Strategies in the Arizona Experiment

Selected information on each full service bidder in the Arizona experiment's first round of bidding is presented in table 7.2, with the bidders grouped by the four bid categories defined in table 7.1[14] For the purposes of discussion, bidders were classified as submitting a "high" bid if their composite bids exceeded the average composite bid of the full service bidders that were judged capable of delivering services and in technical compliance with bidding regulations. A "high capacity" bid was defined as any bid that offered to provide care to more than half of the projected number of indigents in a given county.[15] The composite bids of all providers ranged from 77 to 136 percent of the average composite bid. A part of this variation no doubt could be attributed to different expectations concerning utilization patterns across counties. However, some bidders in multiple counties made no explicit allowance for possible differences in utilization, submitting identical prices in every county.[16] (The submission of a single price may have been an attempt by bidders to minimize bid preparation costs.)

In general, bid prices were higher in rural than in urban areas, possibly reflecting higher expected utilization in rural areas. However, it seems more likely (based on interviews with representatives of bidding organizations) that the higher rural bids also resulted from expectations of less market competitiveness and a greater likelihood of being chosen by the state as a winning bidder. It is also generally true that most bidders throughout the state expected some sort of negotiation to occur over bid prices and capacities. Therefore, the average level of all bids is probably higher than would have been the case if negotiation had been explicitly ruled out prior to bidding.

These general observations on the bidding results provide a perspective for consideration of the bidding behavior of different providers. It is possible to identify four groups of bidders where similar factors appear to have dominated decision making in the preparation of bids: established HMOs, county government delivery systems, rural

Table 7.2 First Round Bidding Results

Bidder/County	Bid/Average Bid[a]			Capacity/Estimated Number of Indigents	Group or Staff HMO	Individual Practice Association[b]		
	All Counties	Urban	Rural			County	Hospital	Other
B₁: *High Price/High Capacity*								
Academy of Family Physicians/Greenlee	1.05		.99	1 +				X
Coconino Health Care/Coconino	1.13		1.06	1.0		X		
Comprehensive AHCCCS Plan/Coconino	1.36		1.28	1.0			X	
Gila Medical Services/Gila	1.02		.96	.56				X
Mt. Graham Community Hospital/Mt. Graham	1.31		1.24	1 +			X	
Western Sun (Community Health Care)/Yuma	1.07		1.01	.63				X
B₂: *High Price/Low Capacity*								
Arizona Health Plan–INA/Maricopa[c]	1.02	1.18		.06	X			
Gila Medical Services/Pinal	1.02		.96	.01				X
Southeastern Arizona Governments Association/Cochise	1.29		1.22	.48				X

B₃: Low Price/High Capacity

Academy of Family Physicians/all counties except Greenlee	.78	.91	.74	1 +		X
Dynamic Health Services/Mohave	.94		.89	1 +	X	
Health Care Providers/ Maricopa	.99	1.15		1 +		X
Pinal	.99		.94	.93		
Maricopa Health Plan/ Maricopa	.91	1.05		1 +	X	
Northern Arizona Family Health Plan/Yavapai	.95		.90	.68		X
Pima Health Plan/Pima	.78	.90		.99	X	
Pinal General Hospital/ Pinal	.82		.77	1 +	X	

B₄: Low Price/Low Capacity

El Rio-Santa Cruz/Pima	.77	.89		.26		X
Northern Arizona Family Health Plan/Coconino	.95		.90	.01	X	
PimaCare/Pima	.80	.92		.04		X

[a] The unweighted average composite bid for all counties was $95.96, with averages of $101.76 in rural counties and $83.02 in urban areas.

[b] In counties where the IPA had affiliations with both county governments and hospitals, the primary affiliation is listed as county government.

[c] The Arizona Health Plan and INA Health Plan were in the process of merging at the time bids were submitted. They submitted identical bids which are treated as a single bid in this table.

hospitals, and newly formed, multicounty individual practice associations.

Established HMOs

At the time of the initial round of bidding there were six established rïMOs in Arizona, all located in the two urban areas: Arizona Health Plan and INA Health Plan in Phoenix; El Rio Neighborhood Health Plan, Pima Care, Intergroup, and INA Health Plan in Tucson. During the period of bid preparation, the two HMOs in Phoenix were in the process of merging. They submitted bids identical in price ($97.56) and capacity (2500), and therefore were treated as a single bidding organization. None of the HMOs fits the typical individual practice association concept of a loose network of solo physicians and single specialty group practices. Instead they are all based on multispecialty group practices providing services through a limited number of clinic facilities.

When formulating the AHCCCS, Arizona legislators expected that the established HMOs would compete actively for indigent patients. This was not the case in the first round of bidding, where two of the HMOs declined to submit a bid and the remainder offered to serve a limited number of eligibles. The HMOs that did bid generally followed a low price, low capacity bidding strategy (the exception, the Arizona Health Plan–INA bid, was only slightly above the average composite price).

There are several considerations that could explain the limited involvement of HMOs in the AHCCCS. First, the facilities of the HMOs are generally not located conveniently for the indigent population. Facility sites were chosen to be attractive to employed groups, which are the primary marketing targets of the HMOs. A commitment to serve a large number of indigents could require that additional space be built or leased in areas where indigents are concentrated and that new personnel be hired to staff them. Second, the HMOs were growing steadily through private sector enrollment, and some expressed concern that the addition of large numbers of indigents could reduce their attractiveness to private employed groups and add to existing growth-related organizational stress. These two factors, together with the experimental nature of the AHCCCS and its limited duration, supported a strategy of limited participation during the initial phase.

The strategy that the majority of the HMOs adopted was to submit low capacity, ''reasonably priced'' bids as a method of preserving future options. Some bidders expressed a belief that, in subsequent rounds of bidding, preference in the selection of winning bidders might be given to incumbent organizations. Participation in the initial phase of bidding therefore increased the likelihood that the HMOs could more readily expand their indigent enrollment in the future, should participation prove to be profitable or should the private group market become more difficult to penetrate. Also, there was concern among some HMOs that the AHCCCS would eventually tie the enrollment of state and county employees by HMOs to participation in the indigent program. Submission of a bid in the initial phase provided protection against this possible future occurrence. Finally, submission of a bid was considered by some HMOs to be important for political reasons. During its inception phase, the AHCCCS program enjoyed broad-based political support in Arizona. HMOs were expected to play an important role in its success. Failure to submit a "good faith" bid would risk the displeasure of key political leaders in the state. The submission of a "reasonably priced" bid demonstrated a "good faith" effort at participation.

In summary, the bidding strategy of the participating HMOs maximized the chances of selection as a winning bidder (low price) while limiting the potential for AHCCCS participation to adversely affect revenues from their private patients (low capacity). The primary objective of this bidding strategy seemingly was to avoid the possible long-term risks associated with nonparticipation rather than to maximize the expected short-run profits from participation. Clearly the objective functions of the HMOs were more complicated than simple profit maximization applied to indigent patients, and the repetitive nature of the bidding process had a significant impact on bidding strategy.

County Government Delivery Systems

Prior to the AHCCCS, each county in Arizona had total responsibility, within state guidelines, for providing and financing acute and long-term care for its indigent residents.[17] One objective of the AHCCCS legislation was to create funding for indigent care that would remove some of the financial burden from counties in the future. Each county's contribution to the AHCCCS in fiscal year 1982–83 was set at 40 percent of the amount it budgeted or expended (whichever was less) on indigent health care in fiscal year 1980–81, to be increased to 50 percent in the last two years of the demonstration.[18] As a result, at least a portion of county expenditures on acute care for indigents became a budgetable item under the AHCCCS, rather than an open-ended commitment, as in the past. The degree to which individual counties benefit by this financing arrangement will vary considerably by county for at least two reasons. First, counties will continue to be responsible for long-term care. Since county contributions to the AHCCCS are determined as a percentage of total county expenditures on all care for indigents, counties with relatively large proportions of fiscal year 1980–81 expenditures devoted to long-term care will benefit proportionately less under the new financing arrangement. Second, the AHCCCS legislation prohibits counties from reducing their services or increasing their eligibility requirements during the demonstration. Thus some counties are mandated to pay for acute care that is not covered by the AHCCCS but was previously available to indigents.

The manner in which individual counties responded to the AHCCCS program, as evidenced by their bidding behavior, depended primarily on the delivery systems they had utilized historically to provide care to their indigent populations. The majority of rural counties had reimbursed hospitals and physicians their billed charges or (less often) flat rates to provide indigent care. Since they were not involved in the direct provision of care prior to the AHCCCS and had no special expertise in this regard, they naturally chose not to participate in the AHCCCS as bidders. The decision making of counties with county-operated medical facilities was much more complicated. Both Maricopa County (Phoenix) and Pima County (Tucson) own large, modern hospitals, while Maricopa County also operated a system of outpatient clinics for indigents. Coconino County, which includes the third largest city in Arizona (Flagstaff), owns and operates clinics serving specific health care needs in its population, and Pinal County, located just south of Phoenix, owns its own hospital.

These counties possessed some historical data on which to base bids and at least some elements of a medical care delivery system. The existing systems were supported by constituencies in the counties and within the county governments themselves. Participation in the bidding process was advocated by these constituencies in the hope that a winning bid would result in a continued flow of patients to county facilities. This, it was argued, would sustain the viability of the county delivery system at least through the demonstration period, a desirable goal given the possibility that the AHCCCS program might be abandoned after three years.

In the urban counties, the dominant consideration in the decision to submit a bid was the potential fate of the county hospital if the county were not a winning bidder. In both counties, virtually all indigents requiring inpatient services were served by county facilities prior to the AHCCCS. Furthermore, the county hospital in Tucson was a major teaching facility for medical students. It was anticipated that private sector bidders would develop contracts for inpatient services with other hospitals, thus dispersing the hospitalization of indigents. Unless county governments were successful bidders and enrolled large numbers of program eligibles, occupancy rates in their hospitals could drop precipitously. Without a county-sponsored AHCCCS plan, county governments would be faced with the prospect of "double payment" for inpatient care for indigents; the fixed costs of the county hospitals, now operated at a low occupancy rate, would continue, while at the same time the counties would be required to fund a portion of the AHCCCS program, in effect paying the inpatient expenses of program enrollees in other institutions.[19] While payments for fixed costs could be avoided by selling the hospitals, the conditions of sale under these circumstances would not be advantageous to the counties. Furthermore, if the AHCCCS program failed, the county commissioners might be accused of "giving away" their hospitals when they were still needed.

Given this environment, both urban counties offered to serve all of the estimated indigents for a relatively low price (a B3 bidding strategy). In essence their bidding behavior exhibited a willingness to trade higher revenues for a lower probability of disaster. It yielded expected surpluses (or losses) that compared favorably to the alternative outcomes associated with not bidding. A low capacity bid would have limited the flow of state and federal dollars to the counties unnecessarily (given existing unused capacity in county hospitals), while a high bid price would have risked losing the contract, with the disastrous (from the county's point of view) consequences just outlined. In fact, the bid prices submitted by the counties might have been lower but for fears about the possible distribution of patients among winning bidders that would result from the enrollment process. County officials were concerned that they would enroll a disproportionate number of past heavy utilizers of their facilities because of familiarity with the facilities, procedures, and staff. Thus their average costs per patient would be higher than expected if enrollees were randomly distributed across plans.

Rural Hospitals

At the time that the AHCCCS was implemented there was concern that there would be few prepaid, full service bidders in rural counties. Instead, multiple full service bids were submitted in nine of Arizona's twelve rural counties. In three counties, the bids identify hospitals in major management roles (Comprehensive AHCCCS plan, Pinal General, Mt. Graham Community Hospital) while in other counties they were actively involved in bid formulation (Northern Arizona Family Health Plan) or accepted considerable risk for hospitalization experience as a subcontractor (Gila Medical Services).

In determining their bidding strategies, rural hospitals were faced with a number of conflicting and complex considerations. The Arizona Hospital Association attempted to facilitate the decision making of its rural members by holding a series of meetings, commissioning a consulting firm to prepare an analysis of bidding options, and recommending consultants to rural hospitals desiring help in preparing bids. Through these activities rural hospitals pooled the cost of identifying and evaluating potential outcomes and their probabilities of occurrence.

From the time the AHCCCS was first proposed, rural hospitals were concerned about the possible effect of the program on their economic viability. One way that AHCCCS providers could reduce costs per enrollee would be by reducing hospital utilization of enrollees.[20] Since rural hospitals serve the entire range of patients in their communities, including significant numbers of indigents, attempts by winning bidders to control hospital utilization would inevitably affect the occupancy rates and finances of rural institutions. Therefore a primary consideration of rural hospitals, in evaluating their options for participation in AHCCCS, was identifying a strategy that minimized adverse effects on hospital balance sheets.[21]

The option of submitting a bid as a full service contractor in the AHCCCS offered several advantages to the rural hospital. As a winning bidder, it could retain control over the hospital utilization of at least some of its existing patients and potentially gain a limited number of new patients. Even if the usage of the hospital on a per enrollee basis were reduced by program participation, at least the hospital would share in the cost savings as the primary AHCCCS contractor. Furthermore, in this capacity the hospital would be able to exercise some degree of managerial control over decisions relating to hospital utilization. Finally, the prepayment aspect of the program could benefit the hospital's cash flow position. Program administrators would transfer funds to the hospital on a regular basis depending on the number of enrollees in the hospital's plan, but independent of the usage of services by enrollees. The hospital would have control over these monies until services were actually utilized.

The disadvantages to the rural hospital of being a full service bidder hinged in part on the uncertain nature of the advantages described above. The profits the hospital would receive from AHCCCS depended on the number of indigents who enrolled in the hospital plan. This, in turn, depended on the number of winning bidders in the county and the methods used by program administrators in allocating patients among plans. The return from being a winning bidder also depended on the accuracy of the cost estimates used in constructing a bid and the ability of the hospital to effectively manage the plan. There was considerable uncertainty in both respects. Data on the use of services by potential AHCCCS eligibles in rural areas were either unreliable or unavailable. More importantly, a hospital full service bidder would be required to assume the risk for outpatient, as well as inpatient, care. Most rural hospitals had little managerial experience in this area. Finally, a successful hospital plan would clearly require the close involvement of staff physicians in management decisions, since physicians exercise primary control over hospital admissions. For some hospitals this required a change in existing administrative procedures. The uncertainties concerning the potential profits from participating as an AHCCCS bidder, along with the developmental and start-up costs associated with plan formation, made the perceived benefits of participation less than compelling for many rural hospitals.

While participation as a bidder was not necessarily viewed as desirable by rural hospitals, neither was the alternative course of action—participation as a subcontractor to a bidder. Their market positions guaranteed that most rural hospitals would be asked to subcontract as providers of inpatient care to AHCCCS enrollees.

For hospitals located some distance from Arizona's urban areas, subcontracting represented a reasonable option. Although their influence over plan management, reimbursement levels, and utilization control efforts was less as a subcontractor, they ran little risk of losing patients to urban hospitals through nonparticipation or of incurring financial losses as a primary contractor.

However, rural hospitals located nearer to Phoenix and Tucson were concerned that participation as a subcontractor would not protect them from patient losses. They feared that the winning bidder would not utilize the full range of services of the rural hospital, preferring to negotiate subcontracts for specialty services with urban institutions. This could jeopardize the practices of some rural specialists and thereby threaten the hospital's census of private patients. Furthermore, the winning bidder could alter hospitalization patterns for common admitting diagnoses as well, favoring hospitals with lower rates or utilizing primary care gatekeeper physicians who preferred to admit at other institutions.

As a consequence, the relative attractiveness to rural hospitals of participation as a full service bidder depended greatly on their perceived vulnerability as a subcontractor. This, in turn, was based on their estimate of the probability that an "outside" organization would be the winning bidder in their county, which could result in the adverse consequences for admissions and reimbursements just described.

Very early in the implementation of the AHCCCS program it became almost certain that an "outside" organization would bid for the indigent contract in the rural counties. The Arizona Academy of Family Physicians, based in Phoenix, indicated that it would form an individual practice association to submit bids in all counties. It stated its intention to utilize hospitals throughout the state, reimbursing them at their normal rates. Hospital expenses for enrollees would be contained by an aggressive program designed to reduce hospital admissions. The Academy was also clear in its plan eventually to market to private sector employees across the state, in addition to providing services to indigents. Concern about the Academy's bid was a major factor tipping the scales in favor of active participation in the AHCCCS for many rural hospitals.

The three hospitals that submitted full service bids offered to serve large numbers of eligibles but at a relatively high price (a B1 bidding strategy). Since each hospital provided essentially all of the inpatient services to indigents in their county prior to the AHCCCS, they did not face capacity constraints in formulating their bids. Indeed, one of the objectives of bidding was to maintain or enhance existing occupancy rates. From the viewpoint of rural hospitals (in contrast to the urban HMOs), indigent patients were complementary to private pay patients. Higher occupancy rates made possible by independent contracts would permit the hospitals to offer a broader range of services, thereby increasing the likelihood that private patients would be hospitalized at their facilities. There are several explanations for the relatively high price attached to the bids. First, the bids were influenced by the stated preferences of program administrators for multiple full service bidders in each county. In the rural areas, the organizations intending to submit bids were well known prior to the bidding, so the hospitals were aware of the state's alternatives in selecting winners. In most cases, it was assumed that a relatively high bid would not seriously reduce the chances of being chosen as a winning bidder. Furthermore, it provided a cushion against the risk associated with a "new venture" by the rural hospital. Finally, some of these hospitals submitted high bids because they expected to negotiate over price with program administrators.

Individual Practice Associations

In its initial year, the AHCCCS stimulated the development of three individual practice associations that bid in multiple counties (Northern Arizona Family Health Plan, Academy of Family Physicians Individual Practice Association, and Health Care Providers). Each consisted of physicians with primarily fee-for-service practices who were reimbursed for indigent enrollees on a discounted fee-for-service basis, with some potential to share in any surpluses generated by their plans. These bidders offered to serve large numbers of indigents with bid prices below average.

The IPAs offered individual physicians a means of participating in the AHCCCS, while spreading the risks of participation and the costs of preparing a bid. While the IPAs hoped to gain financially from the contract, in all three cases there was another objective clearly in mind: enrolling private employee groups at some future time. The AHCCCS legislation specifically included a provision for winning bidders to offer their services to public and private employees, although the means by which this would be implemented were not clearly described. Even without this legislative encouragement, participation in the AHCCCS still provided a vehicle for the development of health plans to the point that marketing to private groups became feasible. For these plans, AHCCCS participation subsidized the costs of developing contractual relationships, instituting and refining utilization review and quality assurance systems, and testing financial control mechanisms. This type of subsidy was particularly desirable since no IPAs (of the type described above) existed in Arizona prior to the AHCCCS. To take advantage of this market opportunity, these organizations set prices low enough to minimize the risk of having their bids rejected. While their hope was to at least break even in the initial and experimental phases of the program, a major objective was to tap the long-run profit potential of employed groups and Medicare eligibles.

To limit possible short-run losses incurred in developing plan administrative apparatus, the IPAs desired to spread the fixed costs of plan development and administration over large numbers of enrollees. Consequently, they bid for relatively large capacities and encouraged program administrators to build enrollment quickly and to assign indigents to their plans. For example, the Academy offered to serve more indigents in each county than the state projected as eligible for the program. After bids were submitted it also argued through the local media that the state should award a single contract to the Academy in order to save the state "between $30 million and $40 million."[22] This strategy, which the state rejected, would have lowered Academy administrative costs per enrollee.

Summary

From the providers' point of view, participation in a competitive bidding process for indigent medical care involves confronting uncertainty at every stage of the decision-making process. For most potential bidders, the costs of providing medical care to indigent eligibles under prepayment incentives are difficult to estimate based on existing data. Potential bidders must make somewhat arbitrary assumptions concerning utilization of services, per unit costs, and enrollment of eligibles (which affects administrative costs per participant). They must devise bidding strategies based on these estimates and their assessments of the subjective probabilities of uncertain subsequent events. Also, there are many possible outcomes associated with each bid, and providers are concerned with the distribution as well as the expected value of potential profits in formulating their bids. Given this bidding environment for indigent medical care, bidding strategies vary considerably across providers and depend on such factors as organizational characteristics, access to information, quality of information, expectations about the actions of competitors and program administrators, and organizational objectives in the short and long run. This variation was illustrated quite clearly in the diversity of considerations given weight by bidders in the Arizona experiment.

The four types of bidders discussed in this chapter focused on different areas of uncertainty in constructing their bids. Established HMOs were concerned with the uncertain effect that enrollment of indigents would have on their ability to attract employed group enrollees and to continue to provide them with expected levels of service at reasonable premium levels. Their desire to maintain access to government employees in the future also played a role in the bidding strategies they adopted. County officials were concerned primarily with the uncertain financial and political impacts of bidding as they related to existing public programs and, especially, county hospitals. Their bidding strategies attempted to minimize the probability of a disastrous outcome. Rural hospitals were forced to assess the uncertain consequences on hospital occupancy rates of participation as a subcontractor versus participation as a primary bidder—where both choices were perceived as unattractive relative to the status quo. The long-term consequences for private patient admissions were particularly difficult to assess but were viewed as potentially important. New IPAs saw AHCCCS participation as a means of developing an organization that would be attractive in future years to public and private employers. The potential, but highly uncertain, profits of future expansion into this market played a major role in determining their bidding behavior.

A great many sources of uncertainty for providers in bidding will become less important as the bidding process is repeated. Over time, more reliable information on indigent costs and utilization of care will become available. As bidding experience accumulates, it will become easier for bidders to predict the bidding behavior of competitors. The criteria that state officials employ in deciding to negotiate with providers and in awarding contracts will become clearer, and their performance in administering the program will become more predictable.

While a reduction in uncertainty will occur over time due to the providers' accumulation of experience, should it be accelerated through actions by the state? One major area of provider uncertainty arises with respect to estimation of indigent medical care utilization and costs. In studying competitive bidding for offshore oil drilling rights, several authors have argued that government should provide information to avoid "socially wasteful" duplicative expenditures by bidders on estimation efforts.[23] The efforts of AHCCCS program administrators to supply providers with information about the indigent population, including data on utilization rates and predicted numbers of eligibles, were consistent with this recommendation. Also, the AHCCCS legislation charged administrators of the program with the responsibility for providing technical assistance to potential bidders, although constraints on time and resources limited this effort.[24] Besides reducing expenditures on estimation, providing information on utilization and costs could yield other benefits to the state, including more provider participation and lower bids.[25]

A second significant source of uncertainty concerns the actions of program administrators in defining and enforcing the "rules of the game.'' In the AHCCCS, rules and regulations were not final at the time of bid submission, nor were criteria for negotiating and awarding contracts made public, in part because of the time constraints on program implementation. Several bidders suggested that these delays created unnecessary and undesirable uncertainty for bidders, leading to inefficient outcomes; Smiley (1979) has observed in his analysis of offshore oil bidding that uncertainty with respect to the government's bid rejection system ''complicates matters for the bidders because they must try to anticipate the government's strategy and adjust their own strategies accordingly. This results in additional uncertainty, which may result in more conservative bidding and higher expenditures on bid preparation.''[26]

A third source of provider uncertainty involves the actual chances of being selected as a winning bidder. Even here, AHCCCS administrators reduced provider uncertainty by stating an intention to select multiple winning bidders in each county. The state took this position in part to induce providers to participate in a new and untried bidding process and to create more potential competitors for subsequent rounds of bidding. However, it clearly is to the state's advantage to maintain some degree of uncertainty with respect to selection of winning bidders. Provider uncertainty in this context motivates the submission of low bids and therefore is essential to the control of program costs through competitive bidding.

Notes

1. R. Engelbrecht-Wiggans, "Auctions and Bidding Models: A Survey," *Management Science* 26 (February 1980): 119–42.
2. Engelbrecht-Wiggans, ibid., notes, "traditional decision theoretic models correspond to games with one player . . . the behavior of any nonstrategic bidders is incorporated into the true state of nature . . . " (p. 21). This simplifying assumption is adequate for the purposes of this chapter, and permits the application of a relatively familiar decision-theoretic approach to the analysis of provider bidding. It is consistent with the early work of Friedman, who treats other competitors as nonstrategic players who follow historical patterns in bidding, and Edelman, who treats all competitors as one entity. See L. Friedman, "A Competitive Bidding Strategy," *Operations Research* 4 (February 1956): 104–12; and F. Edelman, "Art and Science of Competitive Bidding," *Harvard Business Review* 43 (July-August 1965): 53–66. Other authors have utilized game theory to model the strategic behavior of competitors. See, for instance, J. Griesmer and M. Shubik, "Toward a Study of Bidding Processes: Some

Constant Games," *Naval Research Logistics Quarterly* 10 (March 1963): 11–21. A more intricate treatment of competitive strategies along these lines would complicate exposition and add little to the discussion of empirical bidding behavior which follows.

3. The decision tree is presented in collapsed form to conserve space. An introduction to the use of decision trees for management decision making can be found in J. Magee, "Decision Trees for Decision Making," *Harvard Business Review* 42 (July-August 1964): 126–38; and J. Magee, "How to Use Decision Trees in Capital Investment," *Harvard Business Review* 42 (September-October 1964): 79–96. Specific applications of decision trees to descriptions of competitive bidding problems are provided by D. Bunn and H. Thomas, "A Decision Analysis Approach to Repetitive Bidding," *European Journal of Marketing* 12 (1978): 517–28; and R. de Neufville, E. Hani, and Y. Lesage, "Bidding Models: Effects of Bidders' Risk Aversion," *Journal of Construction Division ASCE* (March 1977): 57–70.

4. The introduction of a "research decision" into decision-theoretic structures of this type is common in analysis of marketing decisions. See, for instance, J. Newman, *Management Applications of Decision Theory* (New York: Harper and Row, 1971). The "research decision" is incorporated in a model oil bidding behavior for federal resource leases by T. K. Lee, "Resource Information Policy and Federal Resource Leasing," *Bell Journal of Economics* 13 (Autumn 1982): 561–68.

5. K. Simmonds, "Competitive Bidding: Deciding the Best Combination of Non-price Features," *Operational Research Quarterly* 19 (March 1968): 5–14.

6. The manner in which bidders may incorporate each of these factors in the construction of the bid is discussed in D. Bunn and H. Thomas, "A Decision Analysis Approach for Unique Situation Competitive Bidding," *European Journal of Marketing* 10, no. 3 (1976): 169–75.

7. While it seems reasonable that the state would prefer low prices to high prices, the stated preference ordering for high-priced bids requires comment. It is assumed that high-priced bids with low capacity are desired over high capacity, since they limit the potential impact of high-priced bidders on total program costs. This allows the state to select high-priced bidders, who may be desirable for other reasons, as winners without jeopardizing program budgets.

8. The mechanics of this process are described in detail in J. Magee, "Decision Trees," and "How to Use Decision Trees," and in R. Zeckhauser and E. Stokey, *A Primer for Policy Analysis* (New York: Norton and Company, 1978), pp. 201–56.

9. H. Simon, "Theories of Decision-Making in Economics and Behavioral Sciences," *American Economic Review* 49 (June 1959): 253–83; A. Tversky and D. Kahneman, "Judgment Under Uncertainty: Heuristics and Biases," in D. Wendt and C. Vlek, eds., *Utility Probability and Human*

Decision Making (Boston: D. Reidel Publishing Company, 1975), pp. 141–62.

10. This payoff function is a modification of the approach utilized by Friedman, "Competitive Bidding Strategy," and by D. Baron, "Incentive Contracts and Bidding," *American Economic Review* 62 (June 1972): 384–94.

11. H. Markowitz, "Portfolio Selection," *Journal of Finance* 7 (March 1952): 77–91.

12. For more detailed descriptions and justifications of different decision rules that providers might adopt in making this trade-off, see W. Baumol, "An Expected Gain—Confidence Limit Criterion for Portfolio Selection," *Management Science* 10 (October 1963): 174–82; R. Day, S. Morley, and K. Smith, "Myopic Optimizing and Rules of Thumb in a Micro-Model of Industrial Growth," *American Economic Review* 64 (March 1974): 11–23; and R. Day, D. Aigner, and K. Smith, "Safety Margins and Profit Maximization in the Theory of the Firm," *Journal of Political Economy* 79 (November/December 1971): 1293–1301.

13. For an empirical example, see J. Magee, "How to Use Decision Trees."

14. The data in table 7.2 were abstracted from provider bids on file with the Department of Health Services, State of Arizona. The discussion of provider bidding behavior that follows is based on structured interviews with full service bidders. Most interviews were conducted after submission of bids in the initial round of bidding, but before contracts were awarded.

15. Some bidders submitted bids in multiple counties. If an organization submitted an identical bid in more than one county, that bid is reported only once in table 7.2. Where a bidder submitted bids in multiple counties that differed in price or capacity, those bids are treated separately in table 7.2. Since bids in the urban areas of Phoenix and Tucson tended to be lower than in rural counties, average bid prices are also presented by an urban/rural county classification. Bids submitted by the University of Arizona Medical Center were not included in calculating the averages. The Medical Center occupies a unique position in the state, and is unlikely to have objectives or costs similar to other bidders. The effect of competitive bidding on medical schools and the appropriate role for state-supported medical institutions to play in competitive bidding situations involving the private sector are important policy issues that are not addressed in his article.

16. Substantial variation in bid prices is not unusual in competitive bidding processes. For a discussion of this phenomenon, see P. Crawford, "Texas Offshore Bidding Patterns," *Journal of Petroleum Technology* 22 (March 1970): 283–89.

17. See chapter 2 for a history of the involvement of Arizona courts in indigent medical care.

18. Arizona Health Care Cost Containment System, Senate Bill 1001, State of Arizona, 35th Legislature, 4th Special Session, Phoenix, Arizona, November 9, 1981.
19. B. Action, "Kino Won't Be Closing: Bid Accepted." *Tucson Citizen,* August 31, 1982.
20. Research has demonstrated that this is a primary mechanism by which prepaid health plans contain costs. See H. Luft, "How Do Health Maintenance Organizations Achieve Their Savings? Rhetoric and Evidence," *New England Journal of Medicine* 298, no. 24 (June 1978): 1336–43.
21. This concern was not shared to the same extent by private urban hospitals. Because of the large county hospitals in each urban area, these hospitals did not serve significant numbers of indigents, except in the provision of a few highly specialized services that were expected to continue in some form under the AHCCCS.
22. F. Turco, "Health Care Bidder Claims State Could Save Millions," *Arizona Republic,* September 1, 1982.
23. See D. Hughart, "Informational Asymmetry, Bidding Strategies, and the Marketing of Offshore Petroleum Leases," *Journal of Political Economy* 83 (September/October 1975): 969–85; and A. Smiley, *Competitive Bidding Under Uncertainty: The Case of Offshore Oil* (Cambridge, Massachusetts: Ballinger, 1979).
24. Most providers hired consultants to construct utilization and cost estimates and advise them on bidding strategy. The widespread use of consultants can be interpreted as evidence that providers were willing to pay considerable amounts, in some cases, to reduce this aspect of uncertainty associated with bidding.
25. For a well-developed argument in favor of this view, see D. Reece, *Leasing Offshore Oil: An Analysis of Alternative Information and Bidding Systems* (New York: Garland, 1979). However, Milgrom has suggested that the state can increase its revenues in situations where the high bidder wins by excluding informed bidders. See P. Milgrom, *The Structure of Information in Competitive Bidding* (New York: Garland, 1979).
26. Smiley, *Competitive Bidding,* p. 104.

8

Contract Enforcement and Compliance by Winning Bidders in Arizona

Previous chapters have described the design and implementation of a system of competitive bidding for indigent medical care contracts, as well as provider participation in the bidding process. It will be difficult for researchers to measure the ultimate success achieved by the Arizona experiment in restraining cost increases for indigent medical care, a primary objective of the system.[1] Comparisons with the cost of delivering care under Arizona's delivery system prior to AHCCCS are complicated by differences in benefits and program eligibility and by uneven record keeping by county governments. Comparisons with the costs of traditional Medicaid programs in other states require that a "comparable" population be constructed for research purposes and that state differences in benefits and eligibility requirements be taken into account. Even if such evaluations prove feasible, it would probably not be possible to isolate the cost containment impact of competitive bidding relative to the other cost containment features that are part of the experiment.

Given that a convincing assessment of the impact of the bidding system on costs may not be feasible, in this chapter we turn to other outcomes of the bidding experience. The most obvious alternative measure of performance is the degree to which winning bidders fulfill their contractual obligations to the program. Contractual requirements are an integral part of the bidding process since, theoretically, they allow the state to hold providers accountable. If providers do not meet their contractual responsibilities, then the integrity of the bidding process is clearly compromised. In effect, it is not clear what "product" is encompassed by the submitted bid price and therefore purchased with tax dollars. In the discussion that follows, we review the evidence concerning contract enforcement and compliance in AHCCCS, with emphasis on the first 18 months of the program (October 1982–April 1984). First, we describe the expectations concerning provider performance expressed in the legislation and formalized in the contracts signed with providers. We also summarize the administrative apparatus established by the state to monitor provider performance. Then we review the evidence concerning the contract enforcement efforts of the state and the contract compliance of providers. In this review, we focus on four general areas: subcontractor relations, quality of care/patient grievances, provider finances, and provision of evaluation data. This evidence is discussed in the context of traditional theories of regulation and compared to California's experience in the early 1970s, when it initially contracted with prepaid health plans to provide medical care to indigents.

Contractual Relationships in the Arizona Experiment

The AHCCCS legislation empowered the state government, and in particular the director of the Department of Health Services, to enter into two specific contractual relationships. Of primary importance was the specification in the legislation that "the system shall consist of contracts with providers for the provision of hospitalization and medical care coverage to members."[2] The director was admonished to "require such contract terms as are necessary in the judgement of the Director to ensure adequate performance by the provider of the provisions of each contract executed. . . . "[3] The legislation suggested that requirements relating to financial reserves and grievance and appeal procedures would be desirable. However, it took a very broad view of the types of provider organizations that could enter into contractual relationships with the state, suggesting that contracts be executed with "group disability insurers, hospital and medical service corporations, health care service organizations and any other appropriate public or private persons. . . . "[4]

In addition to the establishment of contracts with provider organizations, the director was required to enter into a contractual relationship with a private firm, selected through a competitive bidding process, to administer the program (see chapter 3). One of the contractual responsibilities of the administrator was the administration and oversight of the contracts that provider organizations signed with the state. In addition, the administrator was to provide technical assistance to providers and potential providers, establish a system of accounts and controls for the system, establish peer review and utilization processes within the provider organizations, and develop a comprehensive system for assuring quality of care. In effect, the legislation limited the activities of the AHCCCS staff within the Arizona Department of Health Services (the "Director") to three areas once the administrator had been selected: (1) supervision of the administrator, (2) review of the provider bids, and (3) award of the contracts.

Provisions of the Standard Contract

The initial step in implementing the required network of contractual relationships was the selection of McAuto Systems Group, Inc. as the administrator in May 1982. A final contract was signed with MSGI in June, and a bidding process to select winning providers was completed in August.[5] During this same time period, MSGI and state AHCCCS staff developed a standard contract to be signed by the winning bidders. For the purposes of this chapter, several provisions of the standard contract are of interest.[6]

Subcontractor Relations. A portion of the contract was directed at relations between the primary contractor (the organization submitting the bid) and subcontractors (entities or individuals delivering care to indigents or providing services to the primary contractor). The primary contractor was held legally responsible for the performance of subcontractors, while the state was absolved of any responsibility if the primary contractor failed to reimburse a subcontractor for services rendered. In addition, the contract allowed the state or the federal government to audit or inspect any subcontractor records regarding services delivered or amounts payable. Subcontractors were required to maintain the necessary records and statistical information required by the state for audits and program management and to provide all reports requested by the state.

Quality of Care/Grievance Procedures. A number of features of the contract also addressed quality of care issues. For example, the contractor was required to (1) maintain a single complete medical record for each member at the site of the member's primary care physician, (2) establish and maintain a system to assure continuity of care (including appropriate referral to specialists, monitoring of ongoing medical conditions, coordinated planning at the time of hospital discharge, and necessary post discharge care), and (3) maintain a system for reviewing and adjudicating complaints by members, including a designated grievance coordinator and informal grievance procedures. To insure that these activities took place, the contract allowed state and U.S. Department of Health and Human Services personnel to inspect all contractor facilities, conduct medical audits, and evaluate the appropriateness and timeliness of services. The scope of the inspections could include the condition of the facilities, the grievance system, management systems and procedures, emergency services, and financial systems. However, scheduled inspections could not occur more than once per quarter, and the state was required to issue medical review reports to the contractor detailing findings and recommendations. Contractors were required to furnish, on a quarterly basis, a summary of all complaints received and actions taken to resolve them.

Provider Finances. The contract addressed provider finances in several ways. Contractors were required to furnish copies of relevant financial reports and other necessary information for audit by the state as requested. On a quarterly basis, it was mandatory for contractors to provide statistical cost data concerning enrollees under contract and a summary of amounts received by third parties for services rendered to enrollees under contract. There were also general provisions in the standard contract that required disclosure of "self-dealing" arrangements and mandated the contractor to provide any information necessary for the state to fulfill its program oversight responsibilities.

Evaluation Data. In keeping with the status of AHCCCS as a "demonstration program" subject to extensive evaluation by the Health Care Financing Administration, provider contracts granted considerable powers to the state and the federal governments for data collection. In addition to the data collection activities already noted above, contractors were required to provide quarterly data on the utilization of medical services by enrollees under contract.

Contract Administration

During September and October 1982, standard contracts were signed between the state and 17 different provider organizations to deliver medical care to indigents. In cases where an organization was a winning bidder in many different geographical areas, multiple contracts were signed with that organization. After the contracts were signed, the responsibility for their administration and for the oversight of providers was transferred to MSGI.[7] MSGI hired a medical director whose duties included monitoring the quality of care delivered by providers, evaluating grievances concerning delivery of care, and working with providers to develop quality assurance systems. In addition, a separate unit was created within MSGI with the responsibility for overall provider management. It dealt with providers on a wide range of issues, in addition to contract compliance, including enrollment practices and disbursements from the state to contractors. Initially, the provider management unit consisted of a director and six plan managers. Each plan manager was assigned responsibility for a subset of system contractors, but also had responsibilities relating to "special groups" of enrollees and their problems.

During the first seven months of the program there was considerable instability within MSGI's provider management and medical care units. The initial medical director resigned from his position on January 31 amidst much controversy (as discussed below). He was replaced by two physicians who served on a consulting basis, while residing in California. Both of these individuals had been active in the design and implementation of the program either as consultants to the state or as participants in the bidding process. The initial director of the provider management unit was dismissed on January 21; this position was filled on a temporary basis by two different individuals until a permanent replacement was hired effective March 16. During this period there was also considerable turnover in plan managers and reassignment of responsibilities within the unit. On March 16, there were only two full-time and two part-time plan managers in place. In the next two months, the unit became fully staffed once again, new protocols were developed for dealing with contractors, a centralized record system was established, and efforts were made to strengthen liaison activities with the medical director(s). However, it was not until nine months had passed in the first contract year that some stability was achieved in the units that had primary responsibility for provider oversight and contract compliance.

Even then, much of the effort of plan managers was devoted to other matters not specifically related to contract compliance. The state's expectations regarding reporting and financial disclosure were unclear to contractors during this period, as plan managers awaited policy decisions concerning what specific aspects of plan performance would be regularly monitored and how this monitoring would take place.[8]

The standard contract contained provisions for disciplining provider organizations who were found by MSGI to be violating the terms of their contracts. Contracts could be terminated, with 30 days' prior notice, for a variety of reasons including (1) failure to pay valid accrued claims of subcontractors within a specified period, (2) failure to provide and maintain quality health care services, (3) failure to abide by applicable laws, rules, and regulations of the Department of Health Services, state of Arizona, and the United States government, and (4) substantiation that the contractor endangered the health of members. In addition, the contract could be suspended if a contractor or subcontractor submitted misleading, fake, or fraudulent information relating to claims for payment or submitted inaccurate or incomplete representations in the bidding process for the purposes of obtaining an AHCCCS contract or for a variety of other reasons. While contractors could be disciplined for a large number of reasons under the terms of their contracts, the exact nature of the discipline the state could enact, beyond contract termination, was not clearly described in the contracts. In fact, during the first year of the program, MSGI took no formal action against contract violations. It was not until after contracts were awarded in the second year of bidding that a provider was sanctioned for noncompliance.

Provider Contract Compliance

By combining interviews with state and MSGI personnel, state files and documents, and newspaper accounts, it is possible to construct an overview of the types of compliance problems that arose in the areas of subcontractor relations, quality of care/grievance procedures, provider finances, and the provision of evaluation data. However, the following discussion is most appropriately viewed as illustrative of contract compliance issues that can arise in competitive bidding systems for indigent medical care, rather than as a definitive evaluation of contract enforcement and compliance in the AHCCCS demonstration.

Contractor Relations with Subcontractors

The relations between contractors (the bidding organizations) and their subcontractors have caused continual problems for AHCCCS program officials. Subcontractor problems first surfaced with the initial awarding of contracts in October 1982. In order to facilitate participation in the bidding process by provider organizations, the state did not require bidders to have formalized subcontracts prior to submitting their bids. For instance, rather general "letters of intent" from physicians were the only requirement for newly formed IPAs to demonstrate service delivery capability at the time of bidding. After the awarding of service contracts, the winning bidders then attempted to convert these intentions into formal subcontracts. In many cases, the resulting service delivery capability was less than had been suggested by material submitted to the state in support of provider bids. In one instance involving a rural county in northern Arizona, the winning bidder (Arizona Family Practice IPA) was not able to develop sufficient service capability as evidenced by signed subcontracts. As a consequence, the award for this county was withdrawn and a new bidding process took place with a contract eventually granted to a different bidding organization.

Once initial subcontracts had been finalized, contractor-subcontractor problems primarily related to the timely payment of subcontractors.[9] In their contracts with the state, the provider organizations promised to reimburse subcontractors in a timely manner. However, in the case of the new IPAs there were financial incentives to delay subcontractor payments. Since contractors receive payment by the state in advance of service delivery, they have control over these funds until disbursements to subcontractors are required. A significant amount of income can accrue to contractors through the management of this cash flow. If reimbursements to subcontractors are delayed, contractors can earn more interest income on state payments. Consequently, throughout the initial year of the program subcontractors continually complained of late payments by contractors that violated their agreements with the state. For instance, two physician subcontractors to AFP-IPA provided documents to the press in support of their claim that payments for eight of their patients had been delayed by about seven months during the first contract year. A hospital administrator, also under contract with AFP-IPA, reported to the press that his facility was due $37,000 in payments, including $20,000 that was delinquent. He stated, "We are a small hospital, with only 110 beds. If we are owed more than $30,000, that really hurts our cash flow."[10] In a more dramatic action, an ambulance company in the Phoenix area temporarily stopped transporting indigent patients, except in extreme emergencies, because of alleged delinquent payments from Health Care Providers (a Phoenix-based IPA) of $20,000 and from AFP-IPA of $60,000.[11]

While contractors generally dispute the magnitude of the "delinquent" payments identified by subcontractors, they do not deny that a significant number of dollars are involved. However, they typically assert that the late payments are primarily the fault of the subcontractors or the state. Subcontractors are at fault because they submit late bills to primary contractors and then expect unrealistically fast reimbursement, or they treat individuals who are not AHCCCS enrollees and then incorrectly bill primary contractors for their care.[12] The state is at fault, according to contractors, when there are errors in the MSGI master list of program enrollees eligible for treatment. Until such mistakes are rectified, contractors do not receive prepayment for these individuals, and therefore subcontractors must wait to be reimbursed for their care.[13]

At the beginning of AHCCCS, a mechanism was established to identify any potentially widespread problem with payments from contractors to subcontractors. Contractors were required to file a monthly report with MSGI that indicated the status and age of outstanding debts to subcontractors. The purpose of this report was to aid administrators in identifying bills from subcontractors that had not been paid within 90 days of receipt. However, at the end of the first year of the program, only 27.6 percent of these required reports had actually been filed by contractors. Instead, MSGI plan managers each attempted to resolve contractor problems on a case-by-case basis.

No formal action was taken against a contractor until January 1984, in the second year of the program, when Health Care Providers was required by MSGI to submit a complete list of all outstanding bills to subcontractors along with a schedule indicating when they would be paid.[14] This request, which Health Care Providers complied with, was initiated in response to subcontractor complaints. The director of MSGI's provider management unit noted that Health Care Providers had many accounts that were "long overdue, and payment has not been forthcoming despite repeated demands. . . . We have had problems of non-payment with other AHCCCS providers, but they have complied after we complained. Health Care Providers is the exception."[15]

Finally, after the state terminated MSGI's administrative contract in a dispute over payments and performance, the director of AHCCCS within the Department of Health Services ordered all providers by letter (March 28, 1984) to bring their payments to subcontractors up to date by April 15. He warned that "after that date, we will begin to levy sanctions and penalties under authority of the AHCCCS rules and regulations."[16] At the same time, program auditors stated that they had no strong concerns over delinquent payments to subcontractors, but that there had been specific instances where plans had exceeded the state's payment limit.

A final issue on relations between contractors and subcontractors surfaced prior to the second contract period (October 1983). Four rural physician subcontractors to AFP-IPA denied signing subcontracts to provide services during the second year, although AFP-IPA had filed signatures, purportedly in their handwriting, in support of its bid. The leadership of AFP-IPA conceded, after a handwriting analysis, that the signatures were not those of the physicians in question but denied that the firm had played any role in falsifying the signatures. AFP's executive director reportedly attributed the discrepancies to a "clerical error" and an "administrative mistake."[17] The state director of AHCCCS termed the allegations "serious" and noted in the press that a contractor can benefit by signing many physicians in its network because this increases the number of patients served by the contractor and demonstrates to the state that it has enough doctors to provide the required medical services. This is particularly important in awarding contracts in rural areas, according to the director.[18] As a result of this controversy, which relates directly to contract provisions prohibiting contractors from submitting inaccurate or incomplete representations in the bidding process, the Arizona attorney general initiated a criminal investigation.[19]

Quality of Care/Grievance Procedures

It is generally acknowledged by almost all parties involved that MSGI did not systematically and effectively monitor the quality of care provided by contractors in the first year of the program to determine if contractual responsibilities in this area were being fulfilled. At the end of the first year contracts, the AHCCCS program director within the state Department of Health Services stated, "We have to intensify our efforts on quality control. . . . It has not had the emphasis it needs to have."[20] The program's deputy director concurred with this judgment and observed that, during the first year, "the resources were put on eligibility, enrollment and payments. The quality of care questions and all that kind of stuff had to take a back seat."[21] In response to criticisms of its lack of action, MSGI's program director acknowledged that "quality-assurance regulations are outlined in provider contracts . . . but no performance audits of these programs have been done."[22]

Several leaders within organized medicine were highly critical of MSGI's lack of quality assurance monitoring of providers under first-year contracts. One past president of the Arizona Medical Association argued that "the concept of self-policing isn't working. If there was someone looking over the provider's shoulder, or over MSGI, maybe the plan would work. But right now, abuses are ignored. There is no quality assurance. . . . Right now, the only thing holding AHCCCS together is a bunch of doctors. The administrative thing is a fiasco. McAuto doesn't use its enforcement power, and they don't even have a full-time medical director."[23] Support for this viewpoint was also expressed by a spokesman for one of the contractors: "The quality of care [of some providers] had not been monitored by McAuto or the State. There are programs [provider groups] that have no system in effect . . . "[24]

While there is substantial agreement that quality of care was not effectively monitored during the first year of the program, there is much less consensus concerning the quality of care actually received by program eligibles. A number of anecdotal accounts of poor care appeared in the press during that period and created a general impression that substandard care was being delivered by providers in violation of their contracts.[25] This impression was reinforced by the resignation of MSGI's first medical director, three months into the initial contract year, amid much controversy. Upon his resignation, the director characterized the system as one that "adversely affects the quality of care of those we want to help," charged that MSGI did not follow up on complaints of patients being denied care,[26] referred to "hundreds of complaints about inadequate and abusive medical treatment received by AHCCCS patients,"[27] and argued that a system to monitor quality of care should have been in place before the program began.[28] MSGI responded that the medical director could not document specific charges, particularly against physicians he accused of malpractice. The legislative chairman of the Arizona House Health Committee supported MSGI's position, noting that the medical director had failed to come up with a plan of action to deal with allegations of poor care.[29] The possibility that AHCCCS enrollees were receiving poor quality care was raised again at the end of the first contract year by the results of a physician survey conducted by the Arizona Medical Association. Of the 1550 physicians who responded to a mailing of 5000 questionnaires, 45.7 percent felt that AHCCCS had a "negative impact" on the quality of care during the first year of the program, while 11.8 percent felt its impact had been positive and 25 percent said there was no impact.[30]

It is not clear how many of these expressed quality of care concerns related to provider performance in the delivery of services or to overall problems in system administration and resulting confusion among patients. A former MSGI administrator observed that, during the first months of program operation, there was considerable confusion on the part of indigents who sought care from their normal providers but were instead referred for eligibility determination and enrollment in a program that was unfamiliar to them.[31] Also, a considerable administrative delay sometimes developed between the time patients were declared eligible for the program and the date on which their names appeared on the master lists of subcontractors.[32] Providers may have referred some indigents to MSGI for clarification when this occurred, leading to indigent complaints about delays in service delivery. This type of complaint, while certainly legitimate, reflected the administrative problems of the program in general rather than any overt lack of provider compliance with contracts.

Several pieces of evidence suggest that the quality of care delivered by providers was at least adequate during the first contract period. At the request of the Arizona House Majority Leader, who had received complaints from three Phoenix area physicians, state staff evaluated 677 complaints filed against one contractor, the Maricopa Health Plan, during its first year. The report found that less than 5 percent (32 in total) of these complaints related to poor medical care.[33] The rest of the complaints concerned patients who were sent incorrect plan identification cards or encountered delays in establishing program eligibility. A second plan, the Arizona Family Physicians IPA, conducted a survey of a sample of its own members and found that 74 percent who had received medical care were satisfied.[34] It concluded, as a result, that quality of care problems in AHCCCS may have received excessive media attention, but also expressed concern that some of its own physicians might not be admitting patients "to the hospital when they should."[35] A third survey was undertaken in November 1983, with a sample drawn from among all Maricopa

County (Phoenix) AHCCCS members. This survey, sponsored by the state, found that 89 percent of those who sought medical care during the first contract year were satisfied with the quality of care, while 72 percent reported seeing a physician on the same day that they requested an appointment. However, the survey results also indicated that substantial confusion existed among AHCCCS members concerning how to obtain emergency care and medical transportation and how to file a formal complaint.[36]

MSGI administrators and state staff cited the relatively small number of written grievances received from program participants as evidence that the quality of care offered by contractors was acceptable.[37] According to an MSGI program director: "Each plan has a quality assurance committee responsible for taking care of complaints. If patients are not happy with their resolution at that level, they can file a grievance and appeal to us."[38] An AHCCCS state director, when questioned about the quality of care during the first contract period, observed that "we're not getting a lot of complaints from patients."[39] However, one program participant who successfully pursued a grievance to its resolution in her favor argued that so few complaints had been filed "because most AHCCCS patients are unable to cope with the three-tier complaint system. Many are illiterate and inarticulate. Many are unable to speak English."[40]

Perhaps the strongest support for the quality of care provided by contractors came in the form of an audit by the Accreditation Association for Ambulatory Health Care, the results of which were published in December 1983. The audit found that "overall, the quality of the medical care provided to AHCCCS patients appears to be at least equivalent to the care rendered by AHCCCS providers to their private, non-AHCCCS patients."[41] However, the audit criticized the majority of contractors for not implementing quality assurance systems and nearly all contractors for failing to maintain unit medical records, both of which were required by their first-year contracts.[42] The audit took place during a six-month period and involved visits to over one-third of the primary care offices of participating physicians. The auditors observed that "they knew of no other state that had conducted such a 'comprehensive' review of the health care provided under their medical care systems."[43] After the audit, letters were sent by MSGI's director of provider management to all primary contractors, outlining the steps that needed to be taken to address contract deficiencies and establishing deadlines for contract compliance.

Provider Finances

Contractors under the first year of the AHCCCS were required to file quarterly financial reports with MSGI, as well as an end-of-the-year financial statement. Of the 17 primary contractors in year one, only seven filed any of their quarterly financial reports. A total of 23.5 percent of these required reports were submitted by all contractors. There apparently were no systematic efforts made by MSGI or the state during the first year to enforce compliance with these financial reporting requirements.

While MSGI did not enforce systematic financial reporting by providers, it did undertake two "financial reviews" of contractors, where potential problems appeared to exist. One of these reviews coincided with a newspaper account based on tape-recorded conversations between two of the principals in Health Care Providers.[44] In their conversations, they discussed the shortcomings of their accounting system and the financial problems of the plan, along with other management issues. MSGI subsequently suspended enrollment in the plan for 30 days and required Health Care Providers to respond to the findings of the MSGI review. Among other problems, the review found: (1) less than half of the $8 million paid by the state to the contractor had been disbursed for patient care; (2) about $1.5 million had been withdrawn from the plan during October and November 1983 by the three principal partners for activities characterized by a governor's aide as "personal use;" (3) excessively high rent was paid by the plan to a business owned by the principals; (4) the plan did not have a financial manager; and (5) the plan failed to provide the required financial statements.[45] The state director reported to the press that "if [the firm] is unable to satisfactorily establish its financial solvency and ability to provide contractually required quality health care . . . Arizona may be forced to take steps to terminate its contract."[46]

While Health Care Providers responded convincingly enough to avert the loss of its contract, the incident underscored the lack of financial oversight of contractors by MSGI prior to its own contract resignation on March 15, 1984. Therefore, in a letter dated March 28, 1984 (see above), the state director ordered all providers to submit any overdue financial reports to the state before April 15 as a preliminary step in an extensive financial audit of contractors. Contractors were again threatened with "sanctions and penalties under the authority of AHCCCS rules and regulations" if they did not comply.[47] However, only two relatively small AHCCCS contractors had submitted all of their quarterly financial statements and reports by the required date. In response, the state imposed no sanctions or penalties, but instead extended the date on which the reports were due until the end of the month. Ultimately, all contractors filed these reports, and a financial audit of the plans was undertaken by an independent accounting firm. The audit revealed that the principals in Health Care Providers had withdrawn $777,801 for "undisclosed purposes."[48]

Provision of Evaluation Data

A significant aspect of the AHCCCS is its importance as a research and demonstration project to be evaluated by the Health Care Financing Administration. To facilitate that evaluation, contractors were required to provide a variety of data, including a separate encounter document for each visit to a provider by an enrolled indigent. As with financial and quality of care data, there were difficulties in achieving compliance with this requirement during the first year of the program. Consequently, HCFA officials threatened to withhold federal funding unless they received encounter data by June 1984, as well as a plan for the timely collection and processing of such data in the future.[49] The first installment of the data was supplied by program officials on May 18, 1984 with the caveat that they did not know what percentage of total encounters between patients and providers had been reported to that date. However, about 20 percent of the encounter documents submitted by providers had been routinely rejected as incomplete or inadequate during the first contract year. Also, while some contractors submitted twice the number of encounter documents projected for them, others supplied only about 15 percent of their estimated totals. Program officials promised to develop new methods to facilitate more effective collection of encounter data in the future.[50]

Subsequent Events

During the first contract year, program administrators devoted relatively little effort to ensuring that contractors supplied the data that would permit a systematic assessment of contract compliance in the areas of payments to subcontractors and the financial management of the plans. Nor were strong efforts made to see that contractors established effective quality assurance systems, or adopted unit medical records, or collected the required evaluation data. The sporadic attempts at contract enforcement that did occur were in response to specific problems, often after complaints against contractors had surfaced in the press. The problems in contract compliance during the first program year were openly acknowledged by program administrators, and more systematic efforts were made to enforce contracts beginning in the second contract year. Specifically, program administrators implemented a combined audit approach that merged the management, medical, and financial areas for audit and reporting purposes. Administrative staff began visiting the offices of each contractor monthly, or more frequently as required, and focused their efforts each month on a particular issue of contract compliance.[51]

Despite the increased efforts of program administrators, several winning bidders continued to experience difficulties with contract compliance. In the early summer of 1984, Arizona's governor described the management of the AFP-IPA as "in utter shambles."[52] On July 9, AFP-IPA was placed under day-to-day supervision by the AHCCCS Division director for failing to submit requested financial documents. Previously, the director had ordered that all of the stock in Health Care Providers be placed in a trust account and had selected an independent management company to take over the administration of that plan.

Also in July, program providers (except AFP-IPA and Health Care Providers) were given the option of extending their existing contracts into the program's third year, if they agreed to contract amendments designed "to tighten reporting requirements and close loop holes that have permitted health plans to break the rules and escape penalties."[53] The medically needy/medically indigent eligibles in Maricopa County (Phoenix), for whom AFP-IPA and Health Care Providers were the only providers under contract, were rebid and additional winning bidders chosen. Subsequent to this action, AFP-IPA filed for reorganization in U. S. Bankruptcy Court (September, 1984).[54] The medically needy/medically indigent contracts held by AFP-IPA and Health Care Providers both were cancelled in the spring of 1985, in part because of the ongoing administrative problems of the plans[55] with Health Care Providers agreeing in April 1985 to be liquidated.[56] In May, AFP-IPA, Health Care Providers, and their major creditors sued the AHCCCS program for $24.5 million in allegedly unpaid bills, charging that mismanagement of AHCCCS caused the financial collapse of the two plans. The suit was described by an AHCCCS spokesperson as "ludicrous."[57] By this time, another AHCCCS winning bidder—Western Sun Associates—had filed for protection in Bankruptcy Court.[58]

Interpreting Contract Enforcement and Compliance Behavior

What is a reasonable interpretation of the early experience with contract enforcement and compliance in the Arizona competitive bidding process for indigent medical care? Certainly, one hypothesis is that the contract administrators were incompetent, or had been co-opted by providers, and that the contractors were unscrupulous and inept. While there is certainly variation in the energies, abilities, and ethics of contract administrators and providers that can affect the execution of contracts, other authors have argued convincingly for an explanation with broader policy implications. Williamson, for instance, concludes that franchise bidding "differs mainly in degree, rather than in kind, from the regulation that such bidding is intended to supplant. . . . " and that "it is at the execution stage . . . that the convergence of franchise bidding to public utility regulation is especially evident." In particular, he observes that "the institutional infrastructure that predictably develops to check dysfunctional or monopoloid outcomes has many of the earmarks of regulation."[59]

If, at the execution stage, the activities of contract enforcement and compliance are similar to those of regulatory enforcement and compliance, then descriptive models of regulatory processes should provide some insight into the Arizona contract experience to date. In discussing the regulation of hospitals, Noll describes a regulatory environment in which regulators try to serve the general public interest but have difficulty doing so because the information they have is uncertain or biased and the interests of the various groups that comprise "society" are more likely to be conflicting than harmonious.[60] Therefore, regulators adopt various second-best "success indicators" to guide their behavior and evaluate their own performance. In general, Noll suggests that regulators are concerned primarily with (1) the extent to which their decisions are overridden by legal action, (2) the response of legislators to their decisions, and (3) the performance of the regulated industry and, particularly, the avoidance of a service or financial failure of a regulated firm. Regulatory agencies attempt to allocate their limited resources in a manner that maximizes their performance as reflected imprecisely by these three indicators.

The counterpart to the regulatory agency in the Arizona experiment is the contract administrator, MSGI, which had the legislative responsibilities to execute the contracts signed by the state Department of Health Services with winning bidders. In addition, as described previously, MSGI had major financial intermediary responsibilities, as well as a legislative mandate to provide technical assistance to bidding organizations. Furthermore, during the implementation of the program, the responsibility for all enrollment activities was shifted to MSGI. While MSGI had some experience as a fiscal intermediary in traditional Medicaid programs, its background did not prepare it for the management of a statewide prepayment system for acute care.

From the beginning of the program, MSGI had severe difficulties in executing its own management contract with the state. The procedures specified in the legislation for enrollment of program eligibles were complicated and highly controversial. Resulting enrollment delays had important financial implications for contractors and for county governments in Arizona. For contractors, delayed enrollment meant that membership did not build as quickly as expected, causing the financial projections on which bids were based to be inaccurate. For the counties, the enrollment delays resulted in greater expenditures for indigent medical care than they had expected, since indigents in enrollment queues continued to seek care from county facilities. Also, county governments were forced to allocate more staff resources to eligibility determination than anticipated, an additional drain on county funds. Lawsuits and threatened lawsuits resulted, some of which named MSGI as a litigant. More importantly, contractors and county governments, along with groups representing the indigent, applied pressure on MSGI by lobbying key legislators and by securing media attention for their complaints.

Faced with these problems during the first six months of the program, the contract administrator responded as predicted by Noll's theory of regulatory agency behavior: it allocated the greatest portion of its resources towards enrollment activities and the improvement of provider payment systems. In doing so, MSGI attempted to secure legislative support by addressing the complaints of the legislators' constituents, while at the same time reducing the probability of a service or financial failure by the contractors. From MSGI's viewpoint, this allocation of resources yielded the greatest benefit. Furthermore, to aggressively pursue contract compliance in reporting and in quality assurance at this stage would have contributed even further to provider, and by extension, legislator displeasure with MSGI performance. This could have jeopardized provider participation in the second round of bidding, a very serious concern in a fledgling program. If the program were not attractive enough in the first year to secure provider participation in the second year bidding process, a system failure would result, with the contract administrator receiving much of the blame.

In addition to these considerations, another factor complicated MSGI's incentives to pursue contract compliance. As the program aged, a record of noncompliance with audit and reporting requirements was established, involving virtually all contractors. Any effort to enforce compliance from a single contractor could have been portrayed as prejudicial by that contractor, thus increasing the potential for the decision to be overturned by the courts. However, action against all contractors simultaneously would have risked a service failure and would have consumed a disproportionate amount of administrative resources.

Just as the general incentives faced by regulatory agencies are useful in understanding the contract enforcement efforts of the administrator, the behavior of the contractors can be understood in the context of economic theories of regulatory compliance.[61] These theories suggest that less than complete compliance will be optimal for regulated firms, and that these firms will engage in compliance activities only to the extent that the benefits of compliance exceed the value of the resources necessary to comply. The benefits that accrue to firms that comply with regulations involve primarily "avoided costs" (such as legal fees, adverse publicity, and financial penalties), which result from enforcement actions by the state.[62] However, compliance in reporting to the state could have the additional benefit of yielding information useful in managing the organization. The costs of compliance are essentially the opportunity costs of the resources that are used in contract compliance activities.

During the first year of the program, the benefits of compliance, as measured in "avoided costs," were judged to be very low in expected value by providers, since the probability that the contract administrator would engage in enforcement activities was low. Also, the opportunity costs of contractor resources were high initially, as contractors formalized relationships with subcontractors and enrolled indigents. These factors together suggest that the optimal level of contract compliance by providers during the first program year was low. This conclusion is reinforced by the strategic concerns of contractors relating to the second round of bidding. Compliance with the financial and patient care utilization reporting requirements during the first year would have aided competitors in constructing their bids in the second bidding process.[63] This additional potential cost associated with compliance reinforced the incentives for contractor noncompliance with respect to at least some contract specifications.

By the time the second round of bidding was completed, the incentives faced by the administrator and the contractors had been somewhat modified. The great majority of indigents were enrolled with a contractor, so that the controversy surrounding enrollment had largely subsided. In its place, media attention was now directed at indigents' accounts of poor quality care or callous treatment by providers, and at apparent discrepancies in provider finances. This press coverage heightened legislative interest in contractor compliance with reporting requirements and therefore increased the benefits to the administrator of devoting resources to improving compliance with this aspect of provider contracts. Federal concerns about the collection of encounter data from providers were also increasing; they culminated in a threat to withdraw federal funding if these data were not collected. This increased the potential for system failure if compliance with the reporting requirement was not improved, and increased the benefits accruing to contract compliance efforts.[64] Finally, the need for the administrator to be responsive to provider concerns was somewhat diminished after the second contracts were signed. These contracts could be extended through the final year of the three-year demonstration at the state's option (with negotiation of third-year rates), thus reducing concern over continued provider participation. Winning bidders in the second round included two new organizations providing services statewide, so that a system failure was less likely if the contracts of particular providers were terminated. All of these factors combined to increase the benefits of contract enforcement activities and reduce the costs, leading to stronger efforts by the state to monitor providers during the second year.

The contractors also found that their decision calculus had changed in the second year of the program. The media attention devoted to the problems of a small number of contractors increased the benefits of compliance for all contractors by making the benefits of "avoided costs" larger. This was particularly true for contractors with intentions to market to private groups. Their reputations could be seriously damaged by adverse media exposure concerning contract noncompliance. This consideration, along with a higher probability of state enforcement action, increased the expected value of the benefits of compliance. At the same time, the costs of compliance were less for most contractors. They acquired experience with plan management in the first year, and subcontractor relations had become more routinized. Thus the opportunity cost of devoting resources to compliance activities was lower than in the first year. And, of course, the strategic bidding concerns that made the disclosure of information undesirable in the first year were much less important to contractors at the beginning of the second contract period, since two years were expected to pass before rebidding occurred. These considerations, taken together, suggest a greater propensity for providers to comply with contractual requirements during the second year of the program.

In summary, standard explanations of the behaviors of regulatory agencies and the firms they regulate seem consistent with the observed behavior of contract administrators and contractors in the Arizona experiment. This suggests that the execution of contracts, a vital element in any competitive bidding process for indigent medical care, will be subject to the same influences, and have the same potential for disappointing results, as regulatory processes.[65] This observation is further supported by the experience of the Medi-Cal program in contracting with prepaid health plans during the early 1970s.

Contract Compliance in the California Medical Program: A Parallel Experience

In 1971, the state of California passed the MediCal Reform Act with the objective of enrolling a significant number of indigents in prepaid health plans (PHPs). It was hoped that the act would "produce a cost effective system with quality controlled through free competition in the marketplace."[66] However, fraudulent marketing practices by the plans, horror stories about denial of treatment and poor quality treatment, and financial mismanagement combined to erode these expectations.[67] Unlike the Arizona experiment, in California there was no competitive bidding system to select contractors, the plans could market directly to potential enrollees, and an option was retained for indigents to be served by fee-for-service providers. However, despite these differences, there have been notable similarities in the experiences of the two states in the execution of contracts with prepaid organizations.

In both states, extensive programs were implemented in a very short time period. In California, "to encourage a rapid transition to the cost saving PHP system, the State executed contracts as quickly as possible with only cursory screening of applications and without pilot experience."[68] By the end of 1972, after one year, the California program had nearly 150,000 indigents enrolled with 21 contractors, only five of which existed before that year.[69] The number of contractors in Arizona in the first year (18) was similar, with only four established HMOs among the participating providers.

As the California program developed through its initial years, ever-increasing media attention to contractor abuses resulted in stronger efforts by state administrators to enforce contracts. For instance, legislation was passed to require public hearings before contract renewal, and stricter standards for contractors were adopted (1975). In 1974 the California auditor general published a study indicating that approximately 50 percent of state payments to 15 contractors went for administrative expenses and profits.[70] The California commissioner of corporations subsequently became involved in a financial audit of the PHPs, and several investigations of the program by state and federal agencies were undertaken.

During the first five years of the program there were six different program directors overseeing the contractors. However, it was difficult to monitor contractor performance, since "State PHP records are inadequate and incomplete . . . the lack of adequate data has obviously affected the State's ability to identify problem areas for responsible monitoring of plans, as well as to manage the program as a whole."[71] In particular, systematic records of consumer complaints apparently were not maintained by the California program, nor were detailed utilization data collected for program evaluation purposes. In the latter regard, Spitz notes that "monitoring an HMO is no small task. The elimination of the fee-for-service invoice makes it even more difficult because the HMO has very weak incentives to supply detailed utilization data to the Welfare Department."[72] Using the California experience as an illustration, he argues that a contractor "need not comply with regulations as long as it appears to be moving towards compliance.[73]

The parallels between the MediCal program's problems in executing contracts with prepaid providers a decade ago, and Arizona's experience with contract enforcement and compliance during the first 12 to 18 months of the AHCCCS are obvious and striking. In fact, in their analysis of the California program, D'Onofrio and Mullen conclude with a list of "danger signals" for program administrators that, in retrospect, appear to be prescient with respect to the Arizona experiment in its initial stages. Among the danger signals they cite are:

1. Poorly developed regulations and monitoring mechanisms for assuring reasonable access of members to PHP services, acceptable quality of care, and effective PHP management— including safeguards against profiteering.

2. Rapid program expansion without detailed prior planning and the development of adequate supportive and regulatory mechanisms at the State level.

3. Approval of PHP contracts without adequate prior screening for evidence of operational and delivery capability . . .

4. Lack of state assistance to PHPs, both financial and technical, during planning, organizational and early implementation stages.

5. Lack of mechanisms to assure direct public accountability by PHPs, as well as by the State, to PHP enrollees and to tax-payers, including disclosure of utilization rates, quality of care reviews, identification of financial interests in other organizations, and additional relevant data.

6. Lack of a range of sanctions and procedures, in addition to contract cancellation, for disciplining PHPs with confirmed violations.[74]

Given that several analyses of the California experience with contract enforcement and compliance are available, it is safe to assume that the implications of this experience were understood by Arizona program administrators.[75] Therefore, the problems encountered in executing contracts in Arizona cannot be attributed solely to the "new and innovative" nature of the program. This provides further support for the argument that fundamental incentives facing contract administrators and medical care contractors influence contract enforcement and compliance behavior and can routinely result in substantial noncompliance with contracts. Thus, problems in the execution of competitively bid or negotiated prepaid contracts to provide indigent medical care are predictable and will be difficult to reduce or prevent.

Summary

The Arizona experiment in competitive bidding for the right to provide medical care to indigents resulted in a set of contracts between the state and winning bidders and between winning bidders and subcontractors. One purpose of these contracts was to ensure that the state received the product for which bids were submitted, a consideration central to the integrity of the bidding process. Contract provisions specified the nature of the information contractors would supply to permit monitoring of their performance and required contractors to implement quality assurance systems. During the first year of the program, contractors did not comply with these provisions, nor did the state engage in significant enforcement efforts. The analysis in this chapter suggests that models of regulatory agency behavior and firm compliance with regulations are useful in understanding the Arizona experience and the problems that appear to be inherent in the execution of prepaid contracts for indigent medical care. While competitive bidding processes may prove useful in establishing reimbursement rates for providers of indigent care, they require that the resulting contracts be effectively executed. This draws state governments into contract monitoring and enforcement activities that have many similarities to more traditional regulatory activities and are subject to similar biases. The complexity of these activities and the factors that influence them have not been fully appreciated by advocates of competitive contracting in indigent medical care programs.

Notes

1. An evaluation study funded by the Health Care Financing Administration has this as one of its objectives. See "Federal Officials Get ACCESS Data," *Tucson Citizen*, May 18, 1984.
2. Arizona Health Care Cost Containment System, S.B. 1001, State of Arizona, 35th Legislature, 4th Special Session, Phoenix, Arizona, November 9, 1981.
3. Ibid.
4. Ibid.
5. For a description of the implementation of the competitive bidding process, see chapter 5.
6. The discussion that follows is based on the contract signed by the winners in the first competitive bidding process. This contract was in effect from October 1, 1982 to September 30, 1983.

7. The description of MSGI contract administration that follows is based on interviews with MSGI staff and with staff of the AHCCCS Division, Arizona Department of Health Services.

8. During the first year there were several reorganizations in the top-level management within MSGI as well as within the Arizona Department of Health Services. For example, in the first two years of the program there were four different directors of the AHCCCS Division within the department.

9. C. Sowers, "First Audits of AHCCCS Providers About to Begin," *Arizona Republic*, April 3, 1984.

10. A. Ariav, "Signatures for Health Plan Not Theirs, 4 Doctors Say," *Arizona Republic*, September 11, 1983.

11. W. LaJeunesse, "Ambulance Firm Refusing AHCCCS Patients," *Arizona Republic*, January 11, 1984.

12. Ariav, "Signatures for Health Plan."

13. W. LaJeunesse, "Former County-Hospital Patients Often Left Without ACCESS," *Arizona Republic*, December 4, 1983.

14. W. LeJeunesse, "Ambulance Firm Refusing AHCCCS Patients."

15. W. LaJeunesse, "Health Firm Faces Loss of Contract; AHCCCS Wants to Hear Tapes," *Arizona Republic*, January 6, 1984.

16. C. Sowers, "First Audits."

17. Ariav, "Signatures for Health Plan."

18. Ibid.

19. A. Ariav, "Health Pact Signatures Are Target of Criminal Probe," *Arizona Republic*, September 12, 1983.

20. A. H. Rotstein, "Assurance of Quality of Care Is Main ACCESS Goal for '83," *Tucson Citizen*, September 28, 1983.

21. Ibid.

22. W. LaJeunesse, "Former County-Hospital Patients Often Left Without ACCESS," *Arizona Republic*, December 4, 1983.

23. Ibid.

24. A. J. Sitter, "AHCCCS Goal Called Money, Not Quality," *Arizona Republic*, October 16, 1983.

25. A. H. Rotstein, "Arizona's ACCESS: A Prototype or a Problem?" *Tucson Citizen*, September 26, 1983.

26. C. Sowers, "Resigning Official Assails Health Program," *Arizona Republic*, February 1, 1983.

27. A. J. Sitter, "AHCCCS Goal Called Money."

28. Ibid.

29. C. Sowers, "Resigning Official Assails Health Program."

30. C. Sowers, "Physicians Criticize State's Health Plan for Poor," *Arizona Republic*, October 13, 1983.

31. A. H. Rotstein, "Assurance of Quality of Care."

32. C. Sowers, "Critical Lists: Lags in Roster Deny Care to Patients," *Arizona Daily Star*, October 30, 1983.

33. C. Sowers, "Few Gripe About Care in AHCCCS," *Arizona Daily Star,* October 28, 1983.
34. W. LaJeunesse, "74% of Poor Patients Say Care OK, Poll Finds," *Arizona Republic,* November 24, 1983.
35. Ibid.
36. Arizona Health Care Cost Containment System, Section 1115 Renewal Request, May 1, 1984, Chapter 6, pp. 64–65.
37. A. J. Sitter, "AHCCCS Goal Called Money."
38. W. LaJeunesse, "Former County-Hospital Patients."
39. A. H. Rotstein, "Arizona's ACCESS."
40. A. J. Sitter, "Patient Goes 'Through Hell' As Enrollee," *Arizona Republic,* October 16, 1983.
41. C. Sowers, "Audit Shows Many Providers Lack Quality-Assurance Plans," *Arizona Republic,* December 26, 1983.
42. Ibid.
43. Ibid.
44. W. LaJeunesse, "Tapes of AHCCCS Firm Renewal Cost-Cutting Plans," *Arizona Republic,* December 26, 1983. In an unusual sequence of events, an indigent enrollee who had filed a grievance against Health Care Providers was monitoring her CB radio while recuperating from an illness. In the process, she intercepted mobile telephone calls between two partners in Health Care Providers. Recognizing their voices, she continued to monitor the same channel, tape-recording over four hours of conversations in a two-month period.
45. W. LaJeunesse, "Health Firm's Funds Siphoned, Audit Says," *Arizona Republic,* March 22, 1984.
46. Ibid.
47. C. Sowers, "First Audits of AHCCCS Providers About to Begin," *Arizona Republic,* April 3, 1984.
48. W. LaJeunesse, "Maricopa County Underbids Rivals, Regains AHCCCS Contract," *Arizona Republic,* August 3, 1984.
49. C. Sowers, "AHCCCS Warned to Provide Data or Lose U.S. Funds," *Arizona Republic,* May 10, 1984.
50. "Federal Officials Get ACCESS Data."
51. Arizona Health Care Cost Containment System, Section 1115 Renewal Request, May 1, 1984, Chapter 6, pp. 57–59.
52. W. LaJeunesse, "Maricopa County Underbids."
53. Ibid.
54. L. Lopez, "AHCCCS Hiking Payouts By 20%," *Arizona Republic,* March 17, 1985.
55. Ibid.
56. "Health-Care Providers Sue State, ACCESS for Unpaid $24.5 Million," *Tucson Citizen,* May 23, 1985.
57. Ibid.

58. "New AHCCCS Pact Hikes Cost $21,400 Per Month," *Arizona Republic*, July 13, 1985.

59. O. E. Williamson, "Franchise Bidding for Natural Monopolies—In General and With Respect to CATV," *Bell Journal of Economics* 7 (Spring 1976): 74, 81, 101.

60. R. G. Noll, "The Consequences of Public Utility Regulation of Hospitals," in *Controls on Health Care* (Washington, D.C.: Institute of Medicine, National Academy of Sciences, 1975), pp. 25–48. Noll's discussion of regulatory incentives has also been applied to the nursing home industry. See J. B. Christianson, "Long-Term Care Standards: Enforcement and Compliance," *Journal of Health Policy and Law* 4 (Fall 1979): 414–34.

61. See, for instance, W. K. Viscusi and R. J. Zeckhauser, "Optimal Standards With Incomplete Enforcement," *Public Policy* 27 (Fall 1979): 437–56; G. Stigler, "The Optimum Enforcement of Laws," *Journal of Political Economy* 78 (May/June 1970); 526–36; B. Singh, "Making Honesty the Best Policy," *Journal of Public Economics* 2 (July 1973): 257–63.

62. W. K. Viscusi and R. J. Zeckhauser, "Optimal Standards."

63. For a discussion of the implications of this issue for the performance of competitive bidding systems, see V. P. Goldberg, "Competitive Bidding and the Production of Precontract Information," *Bell Journal of Economics* 8 (Spring 1977): 250–61.

64. C. Sowers, "AHCCCS Warned to Provide Data."

65. A more general analysis leading to this conclusion can be found in V. P. Goldberg, "Regulation and Administered Contracts," *Bell Journal of Economics* 7 (Autumn 1976): 426–48.

66. C. N. D'Onofrio and P. D. Mullen, "Consumer Problems With Prepaid Plans in California," *Public Health Reports* 92 (March-April 1977): 123.

67. B. Spitz, "When a Solution Is Not a Solution: Medicaid and Health Maintenance Organizations," *Journal of Health Politics, Policy and Law* 3 (Winter 1979): 497–518.

68. D'Onofrio and Mullen, "Consumer Problems."

69. Spitz, "When a Solution Is Not A Solution."

70. Ibid., pp. 512–13.

71. D'Onofrio and Mullen, "Consumer Problems," p. 125.

72. Spitz, "When a Solution Is Not A Solution," p. 513.

73. Ibid.

74. D'Onofrio and Mullen, "Consumer Problems," pp. 132–33.

75. Interviews with program administrators support this assumption.

9

The Implications of the Arizona Experience in Competitive Contracting

Over the past several years, states have faced increasing fiscal pressures to alter their indigent medical care programs in order to contain program costs. One of the changes adopted in several states, and under consideration in others, involves selective contracting with providers through some form of competitive bidding or proposal solicitation process in which winners are chosen based on bid prices and other criteria. The states hope that the competitive incentives introduced through these selection processes will restrain provider fees and charges, as well as induce the adoption or development of innovative cost-saving approaches to medical care delivery. States with traditional Medicaid programs also expect that limiting participant access to providers under contract will restrain costs by reducing the incidence of expensive "doctor shopping." While cost savings from selective provider contracting processes have yet to be conclusively demonstrated in most programs, states have found that these processes are both politically controversial and technically complicated to implement and administer.

In this book, we have examined the competitive provider selection process adopted in one state—Arizona—in considerable detail. The contracting process implemented in Arizona is arguably the most comprehensive in scope and ambitious in objectives of any such state initiative. At the broadest level of generalization, the Arizona experiment demonstrates how rapidly selective contracting processes can accomplish changes in the organization and delivery of medical care. Prior to institution of competitive bidding in its indigent medical care program, Arizona had four prepaid organizations in Tucson, two in Phoenix (those were in the process of merging), and none in the other 12 counties of the state. Physicians in the state were generally considered to be conservative in their attitudes towards prepayment, with a relatively small proportion having had any experience in a prepaid practice setting. However, as in other states, the numbers of physicians per capita and hospital beds per capita were increasing in Arizona; physicians and hospitals were expressing concern over their ability to secure adequate numbers of patients.

The implementation of the initial AHCCCS competitive bidding process in effect created 14 new prepaid organizations in less than eight months. Furthermore, when it was completed, there were prepaid plans in operation in every county in the state. The contracting process also generated several hospital/physician staff cooperative ventures and resulted in major changes in county health care systems. It increased the level of provider understanding of differences among patients in the utilization of services and costs, and exposed a large number of Arizona physicians to prepaid practice incentives.

While the Arizona experience demonstrates to health policy-makers that competitive contracting can be a potent force in stimulating delivery system change, the ultimate impact of that change depends on a variety of factors. Obviously, of foremost importance is the ability of the new organizations to deliver medical care of an acceptable quality while maintaining their financial viability. The Arizona experience in this regard has been mixed, at best. As noted in chapter 8, several winning bidders including the organization with the largest number of AHCCCS patients have experienced severe financial difficulties and been criticized for their poor management and lack of quality assurance activities. Unless they are able to correct these problems and improve the public's perception of their performance, their ability to market services in the private sector will be severely impaired. This is particularly important since, if the impact of AHCCCS on the state's medical care delivery system is to be long lasting, at least some of the winning bidders must make the transition from organizations serving solely indigent populations to effective competitors for private sector enrollees. Several of the contractors are now attempting to make this transition, but their attractiveness to employed groups has yet to be determined.

At a less general level, the Arizona experiment has identified several important issues for state policymakers relating to the design and execution of selective contracting processes. Based on the analysis in this book, it is possible to address several of these issues with specific comments and recommendations. Our recommendations are organized into three categories, corresponding to different phases of the competitive contracting process: design, implementation, and administration.

Design

Issues related to the design of competitive contracting systems for indigent medical care are not likely to receive the attention they deserve from state legislators or program administrators. Legislators tend to regard competitive contracting for medical care as a natural extension of the straightforward bidding processes used in other state procurement decisions. To the extent that they acknowledge design issues, they are likely to delegate their resolution to program administrators. Administrators, however, quickly become immersed in, and overwhelmed by, the day-to-day demands of implementing a new program. By training and by inclination they are inclined to view program administration, and not program design, as their primary responsibility. Therefore, design decisions are often made hurriedly in response to specific crises, without thoroughly exploring their long-run implications. As a result, it sometimes becomes necessary to alter essential design features during the course of implementing and administering the bidding process. This can create confusion and uncertainty among potential bidders and convey to the legislature and the media the impression of administrative incompetence. Consequently, submitted bid prices may be unnecessarily high and confidence in the ability of the bidding process to contain costs may be diminished.

There is clearly no single bidding system design that dominates under all circumstances; the appropriateness of any given design depends in part on the overall environment in which bidding takes place. Also, different designs will frequently imply different trade-offs among policy objectives such as quality, cost, and access. Therefore the recommendations that follow identify areas of bidding system design that deserve special attention because of their potential importance to program performance, but do not advocate the adoption of specific design features. It is hoped, however, that they will focus the attention of policymakers on the design phase of competitive contracting processes.

Requirements for Potential Bidders

Any competitive bidding process must specify the qualifications that are required of organizations in order to participate. Decisions in this area have broad implications for subsequent program performance and should be made after careful evaluation of the bidding environment and program objectives. In the Arizona experiment, a decision was made to require few qualifications of potential bidders. This decision was consistent with the existing environment. There were relatively few established prepaid organizations in Arizona, and they were not able to expand rapidly enough to serve even a substantial minority of the indigents eligible for the program. Therefore, to secure sufficient service capacity, it was necessary to rely on bidding organizations with no records of past performance in the delivery of prepaid care. Also, "opening up" the bidding process to new, untried organizations was consistent with the dominant program objective— the containment of costs. It was hoped that, by increasing the number of potential bidders, spirited price competition would result and program costs would be reduced.

As noted above, this strategy was successful in inducing providers to participate in the bidding process and probably resulted in lower bids than otherwise would have been the case. However, it had predictable longer run consequences for program performance. As described in chapter 8, several newly formed entities that won contracts after submitting relatively low bids subsequently experienced financial and managerial difficulties. Their substandard performance caused continual problems for program administrators and participants. Thus, the lower bid prices that may have resulted from imposing few restrictions on participating organizations were offset, at least partially, by higher administrative costs and diminished legislative and public confidence in the program.

The Arizona experiment does not necessarily suggest that stricter limitations should be placed on potential bidders. However, in cases where limitations on participation are not feasible, it is essential that program administrators devote time and effort to providing technical assistance to bidders before and after contracts are awarded and to monitoring performance and enforcing contract provisions consistently. (This point is discussed further below.) Where a substantial number of existing prepaid plans are potential bidders, stricter qualifications on participation in the bidding process can be imposed, with the likelihood that fewer resources will be needed for technical assistance and the resolution of contract disputes.

Reimbursement of Winning Bidders

In the AHCCCS bidding process, each winning provider group was reimbursed at the amount of its bid. Relative to other questions concerning program procedures, this design decision was made with comparatively little debate. Yet the reimbursement rule adopted in a competitive bidding process has important implications for provider participation and program cost. Furthermore, it is not clear that the reimbursement approach adopted by the AHCCCS is preferable along either of these dimensions.

Under the AHCCCS reimbursement rule, providers who believe they have lower costs than their competitors have an incentive to outguess the competitive process by submitting bids that exceed their true costs. Low-cost providers under this system are rewarded both for their cost effectiveness and for their ability to successfully "game" the system in submitting bids. This incentive to game the bidding process can be largely eliminated by reimbursing all winning bidders at the level of the highest winning bid, or the lowest excluded bid if only one winner is chosen. This procedure results in the payment of a single price for the defined set of services if more than one bidder is awarded a contract. There is no incentive for low-cost bidders to pad their bids since padding does not increase their profits if they are selected and does increase the risk of not being selected.

While it would appear that a "single-price" reimbursement rule would result in higher program costs, this is not necessarily true. Because of provider incentives to pad bids, total expenditures by the state under the rule chosen by AHCCCS officials could exceed the expenditures required to reimburse all bidders at the highest acceptable bid, assuming that all potential bidders are aware of the single-price reimbursement procedure prior to submitting their bids. The existing experimental and empirical evidence concerning the probable relative costs of the two reimbursement options is limited and is not based on experience related to medical care. Therefore, it does not provide clear guidance concerning which approach is preferable.

The single-price reimbursement rule received little attention in the design of AHCCCS because it was perceived to have several practical drawbacks. For instance, AHCCCS officials were advised by legal counsel that an exception to existing state procurement laws would have to be legislated to reimburse providers in amounts exceeding their bids. More importantly, reimbursement of all providers at the level of the highest winning bid gives the appearance of wastefulness on the part of program administrators and political supporters. Nevertheless, this and other approaches to the reimbursement of winning bidders deserve closer scrutiny in the design of bidding systems. The obvious incentives of bidders to "game" the system when they are reimbursed at their bid prices undermines confidence in the bidding process and can lead to administrative actions that reduce its cost-containment potential (as discussed below).

Determination of System Capacity

In the AHCCCS, bidders were allowed to restrict the total number of enrollees that they would accept if selected to provide services. Where the low bid specified a capacity that was less than the estimated number of enrollees in a given geographic area, it was necessary for program officials to select more than one winning bidder. Even when the capacity specified in the lowest acceptable bid was sufficient to serve the projected indigent population, AHCCCS officials preferred to choose multiple winners in as many counties as possible for several reasons.

First, key legislators supported the concept of consumer choice on philosophical grounds. They were particularly concerned that a private sector bidder be available, if possible, when a county-sponsored plan was offered, even if excess system capacity resulted. Then indigents could exercise preferences with respect to provider location and reputation, even though they would perceive no differences in prices and benefit packages among the winning provider groups.

Excess capacity was also viewed as a useful hedge against the adverse consequences of the financial collapse of a winning provider group. This concern proved well founded, as several large providers in the Arizona experiment did encounter financial difficulties. The presence of other winning bidders helped to maintain at least some continuity in the care received by indigents when provider contracts were terminated.

A final justification for choosing multiple winning bidders to create excess system capacity was perhaps the most important to AHCCCS administrators—it would induce more providers to participate in the bidding process. Provider participation was essential to carry out the Arizona experiment in any form and, prior to the initial round of bidding, there was great concern that it would not be forthcoming.

The creation of excess system capacity through the selection of multiple winning bidders has one serious drawback. In environments where the number of potential bidders is limited, it reduces the necessity for bidders to submit low bid prices to win contracts and encourages the "gaming" behavior previously discussed. For instance, in the initial round of bidding in Arizona, 17 of the 20 organizations submitting bids were awarded contracts. If the number of potential bidders in the environment is large, multiple winning bidders can be chosen without seriously compromising incentives to submit low bids, since there is still a significant probability of not being awarded a contract if the submitted bid price is "too high."

Implementation

The implementation of the competitive bidding process, as well as the Arizona experiment as a whole, took place during the first ten months in 1982. As described in chapters 5 and 6, the implementation process was controversial and complex, and the resources available for implementation were quite limited. In addition to encountering problems that are common to the implementation of all innovative public sector programs, the implementation in Arizona also uncovered political liabilities relating to competitive bidding for indigent medical care. In this section of the chapter, we make several recommendations to policymakers concerning the implementation of competitive bidding processes, based on our analysis of the problems encountered in Arizona.

Plan for an Extended Implementation Period

Ten months was an insufficient period of time in which to implement the competitive bidding process in Arizona. In testifying before a Congressional oversight panel, the Governor of Arizona observed, with respect to AHCCCS, that "the start-up period was far too short. The systems needed to manage a health-care-delivery program for 180,000 Arizona recipients were immature and untested. We had difficulties in establishing and qualifying health-care plans, implementing uniform accounting requirements, obtaining necessary financial reports.''[1] Several unanticipated problems arose that contributed to the inadequacy of the original implementation time frame. While these problems (described in chapters 5 and 6) may be unique to the Arizona experiment, it seems likely that any attempt to implement competitive bidding for indigent medical care will encounter unexpected barriers.

The failure to budget sufficient time to address unexpected implementation problems can have important long-run impacts on program performance. In Arizona, it resulted in the undesirable overlapping of implementation activities and the commitment to courses of action without adequate reflection on the part of program administrators. As a result, there was unnecessary confusion and uncertainty among providers and program eligibles. Implementation of the bidding process over a longer time period would have allowed administrators to schedule activities in an orderly fashion and to provide technical assistance to potential bidders. The result would have been a reduction in bidder uncertainty and, potentially, broader provider participation, lower bids, and fewer subsequent problems with the performance of winning bidders.

Maintain an Orderly Implementation Process

Assuming that sufficient time has been allowed for implementation, it is important that implementation activities logically build on each other. This creates a sense of program momentum, permits input from knowledgeable parties, and increases the confidence of providers in program administrators. In part because of time limitations, implementation of the Arizona competitive bidding process did not move forward in an orderly fashion. For example, the rules and regulations governing the program were not complete at the time bids were requested from providers. Nor was an objective instrument for evaluation of bids completed until the very day that provider bids were received. Ideally, both of these implementation activities should have been completed and the results publicized prior to requesting bids from providers. By not fully developing the "rules of the game" before initiating the bidding, program administrators again created uncertainty among bidders, may have inflated bid prices, and probably reduced legislative and bidder confidence in the administration of the program. These factors ultimately contributed to a decison by program administrators to jeopardize the cost containment incentives in the bidding process by negotiating with bidders after bids were submitted (as discussed below).

Be Prepared to Accept the Results
of the Bidding Process

To implement a competitive bidding system that will effectively create long-term incentives for cost containment, the state must be willing to accept the program costs that result from the bidding process as the lowest possible within the limits of acceptable medical practice and prevailing market conditions. This means the state must be committed to funding the system at the level of the winning bids, rather than attempting to force these bids to fit, in total, within some predetermined budget figure. If policymakers believe that expenditures on indigent medical care under competitive bidding are excessive, there can be only two broad options to pursue: reducing the comprehensiveness of future benefit packages, or tightening eligibility requirements. Any attempt to reduce costs by tinkering with bidding outcomes after the fact destroys the essential validity of the process, leads to provider attempts to game the system by padding bids, and thereby severely impairs its potential to contain costs in the future.

It is important that public officials possess sufficient confidence in the incentives of any competitive bidding system to accept its outcomes and face the difficult choices that this might imply for indigent medical care. This requires that they be willing to relinquish the appearance of short-run control of provider reimbursements and overall program budgets, while possibly undertaking unpopular program revisions at the same time, in return for the untested potential for longer term cost restraint promised by the competitive bidding process.

In the Arizona experiment, legislators and program administrators lost some of their confidence in the ability of competitive bidding to contain costs, in part because of the implementation problems they encountered. As a result, they attempted to negotiate with bidders in order to reduce their bid prices. While negotiation may be effective the first time it is employed, it inevitably creates perverse incentives for subsequent rounds of bidding. When negotiation is anticipated by bidders, there are weaker incentives for them to submit low bids.

Since a bidding process that allows subsequent negotiation encourages the submission of excessively high bids, any savings that are generated through negotiation after bid submission must be considered suspect. In this regard, there was a strong feeling expressed in interviews with bidders and program officials in Arizona that at least some bidders anticipated negotiation after bid submission and included a margin in their bids that would be given up in the negotiation process. Nevertheless, negotiation has an undeniable political allure for program administrators. When high bids are brought down to "acceptable" levels through tough negotiation, the negotiators can point to savings that resulted from their "hard-nosed" management of the program. In Arizona, AHCCCS officials claimed that the pseudonegotiation process they employed saved the state from $4 to $5 million.

Administration

Competitive bidding processes do not end with the selection of the winning bidders. After contract awards are made, program administrators must monitor the performance of providers and enforce compliance with the terms of the provider contracts. If providers do not comply with their contracts, then the integrity of the entire bidding process is compromised. Indeed, the purpose of developing formal contracts with winning bidders is to ensure that the state receives the product for which bids were solicited.

The administrative activities of provider monitoring and contract enforcement are quite similar to regulatory activities. As a consequence, they are subject to the same sorts of political and technical considerations that can influence the development and conduct of regulation. For this reason, our recommendations to state policymakers with respect to the administration of competitive bidding processes in the post-award period are similar to several current proposals for regulatory reform.

Avoid Unnecessary Dispersal of Administrative Authority

The responsibility and authority for developing provider contracts, monitoring performance, and enforcing standards should be clearly defined. Dispersal of this responsibility and authority is confusing to contractors, requires the allocation of administrative resources to coordinating activities, and interferes with timely decision making.

In Arizona, the legislative decision to divide responsibility for program administration between a private firm and the Arizona Department of Health Services was based in part on the limited duration of the program. Arizona legislators did not want to develop an agency of substantial size within the executive branch of government that might function as an interest group in support of program extension at the end of the three-year period. Also, several key legislators believed that the private sector was inherently more efficient than the public sector, and that contracting out some of the program's administrative responsibilities was one means of gaining access to private sector managerial expertise.

In practice, the fragmentation of responsibility substantially complicated the administration of the competitive contracting process. For instance, the actual division of responsibilities between the contract administrator and the state was never totally clear, and resolving boundary disputes drained energy and resources from contract management activities. Also, winning bidders were able to utilize this confusion to delay the provision of information required by their contracts and to "appeal" to the state for relief from decisions made by the administrative firm, and vice versa. These sorts of problems developed during the implementation period, were never resolved, and ultimately contributed to the termination of the state's contract with the private administrator. They suggest that the dispersal of administrative authority in competitive bidding processes should, in general, be avoided.

Define Clear Procedures for Monitoring and Enforcing Contract Compliance before Contracts Are Awarded

Procedures to monitor provider performance and gather the information required under provider contracts should be fully developed and in place prior to the selection of winning bidders to ensure there is no confusion when contracts are signed. Contract monitoring should begin immediately so that comparable information is available over time on the performance of all winning bidders. This did not occur in the Arizona experiment. Procedures for monitoring quality of care and securing the timely submission of financial reports were not developed prior to the selection of winning bidders. Turnover and instability within the administrative unit with contract management responsibility delayed the development of these procedures and resulted in inconsistent, sporadic attempts to enforce reporting requirements.

One consequence of this administrative failure was that, when problems arose with respect to the performance of specific providers, program administrators were unable to respond effectively to them.

They had difficulty in determining if performance problems reflected overall program shortcomings, or if they were unique to the contractor in question. The necessary data to answer this question, or to create a strong legal case against providers suspected of substandard performance, were unavailable.

Once a pattern of nonenforcement of contract requirements by program administrators was established, it was difficult to alter. The balance of power between winning bidders and program administrators shifted after enrollments in plans began to build and plans developed their own political constituencies. Then, plans were able to resist the efforts of administrators to enforce contract requirements by labelling these efforts as prejudicial harassment and mustering their political supporters in opposition. Under these circumstances, the threat of contract termination or nonrenewal as a penalty for noncompliance was not credible. In the Arizona experiment, a major program administrative reorganization was necessary, including the termination of the private firm's administrative contract, to break this impasse and facilitate more effective monitoring and enforcement activities on the part of the state.

Develop a Range of Sanctions
for Noncompliance

Ultimately, program administrators must have the power to terminate contracts if winning bidders do not satisfy their contractual responsibilities. However, once providers have enrolled significant numbers of indigents in their plans, this sanction becomes less useful for securing contract compliance. Except under extreme circumstances, program administrators will hesitate to terminate contracts because this can disrupt the continuity of care received by indigents and result in complaints from enrollees and, consequently, from legislators. In Arizona, there was considerable evidence of substandard performance by a few winning bidders (chapter 8), but this did not result in the termination of their contracts during the first two years of the program. Even after some organizations declared bankruptcy, they continued to provide services to indigents. Through a series of administrative actions, enrollment in these plans was reduced over time, in order to minimize the impact of contract termination. Contractual ties formally ended only after this had been accomplished.

Program administrators require a full range of sanctions, including financial penalties, in order to secure compliance with contracts on an ongoing basis. Without these sanctions, winning bidders can be relatively unresponsive to contract enforcement activities, since no single instance of noncompliance is likely to be important enough to merit contract termination. Where a range of sanctions is present, and sanctions are consistently applied, the severity of the penalty can be tailored to the significance of the contract infraction, thereby increasing the credibility and effectiveness of enforcement activities.

Develop Contingency Plans for Contract Terminations

In any competitive bidding process for indigent medical care it seems likely that one or more winning bidders will subsequently incur substantial financial losses or for other reasons be incapable or unwilling to fulfill the terms of their contracts. Program administrators should plan for this possibility so that, if it occurs, enrollees continue to receive care with minimum disruption. In the Arizona experiment, a key element in planning for contract terminations was the decision to select multiple winning bidders in as many counties as possible. This created some additional capacity and thereby facilitated an orderly transition period for indigent patients. Beyond this, however, program administrators should develop "disaster plans" that can be implemented as needed. These plans should, at a minimum, identify the activities to be undertaken upon the termination of a contract, assign staff members the responsibility for each activity, and establish a schedule for their completion. By explicitly developing a course of action prior to the event, program administrators can be better prepared to act decisively when providers voluntarily withdraw from their contracts or when contract termination is appropriate because of inadequate performance.

Conclusions

The analysis of the Arizona experience contained in this book raises far more issues than it can address. For health policy analysts, the issue of effective bidding system design remains largely unexplored. As chapter 4 suggests, there are a number of alternatives that might be adopted, each implying somewhat different incentives for participating bidders. While laboratory experiments hold some potential for assessing the properties of these alternatives, experiments that capture the essential characteristics of indigent medical care programs have yet to be conducted.

A second issue of interest to health policy analysts, as raised by the analysis of the Arizona experiment, is: How should contract enforcement activities be structured and carried out to ensure the best possible results? Certainly the experiences in Arizona and previously in California suggest that this will be a difficult task. However, the enforcement of public contracts with the private sector is common in a variety of areas, including construction, defense, and research. A careful examination of the development of contract enforcement in these areas could suggest strategies that advance the very basic recommendations offered in this chapter.

In addition to these and similar issues of program design and administration, the Arizona experience raises research questions concerning provider behavior. For instance, how will provider organizations change and mature as contracting processes mature? Which organizations will survive and which will fail? Will the incentives facing contracting organizations be strong enough to induce them to develop or adopt innovative, cost-effective approaches to medical care delivery? Will prepaid organizations with exclusively indigent medical care contracts be able to effectively market to the private sector as well? If so, which organizations will be able to successfully expand into the private sector, and why will they be successful? The variety of competitive contracting processes already implemented or under development by the states will provide an exceptional opportunity for health care researchers to study the behavior of providers as they respond to diverse incentive structures and new market opportunities. The results of this research will have important implications for the future refinement of selective contracting with medical care providers.

Notes

1. W. LaJeunesse, "Injection of Cash, New Blood Braces AHCCCS For Third Year of Experiment," *Arizona Republic*, September 30, 1984.

Index

About the Authors

JON B. CHRISTIANSON is a professor in the Department of Management and Policy and the Department of Economics at the University of Arizona. He is an economist whose research interests include the design, implementation, and evaluation of cost-containment policies in medical care, as well as the response of providers to such policies. Professor Christianson received a bachelor's degree in mathematics and economics from St. Olaf College and a master's degree and doctorate in economics from the University of Wisconsin–Madison. Prior to joining the faculty at the University of Arizona, he was an associate professor in the Department of Agricultural Economics and Economics at Montana State University. Other monographs coauthored by Professor Christianson include *Health Care Policy: A Political Economy Approach*, *Informal Care of the Elderly*, and *Current Strategies for Health Care Expenditures*.

DIANE G. HILLMAN is a research specialist in the Department of Management and Policy at the University of Arizona. She has published in the areas of biomedical research, rural health care delivery, and health policy and has worked extensively with health policy makers at the state level. Ms. Hillman received a bachelor's degree in biology from the University of Rochester, a master's in biology from the State University of New York at Buffalo, and a master's of public administration from the University of Arizona. Her prior professional responsibilities have included the development of a rural health plan for the State of Arizona and the conduct of research on the biochemical genetics of inherited disease.